Roy Williams

Sucker Punch

Methuen Drama

Published by Methuen Drama 2010

1 3 5 7 9 10 8 6 4 2

Methuen Drama
A & C Black Publishers Limited
36 Soho Square
London W1D 3QY
www.methuendrama.com

ISBN 978 1 408 13136 7

A CIP catalogue record for this book is available from
the British Library

Typeset by MPS Limited, A Macmillan Company
Printed and bound in Great Britain by
CPI Cox & Wyman, Reading, Berkshire

ROYAL COURT

The Royal Court Theatre presents

SUCKER PUNCH

by **Roy Williams**

First performance at The Royal Court Jerwood Theatre Downstairs, Sloane Square, London on Friday 11 June 2010.

SUCKER PUNCH

by Roy Williams

in order of appearance
Charlie **Nigel Lindsay**
Tommy **Jason Maza**
Leon **Daniel Kaluuya**
Troy **Anthony Welsh**
Becky **Sarah Ridgeway**
Squid **Trevor Laird**
Ray **Gary Beadle**

Director **Sacha Wares**
Designer **Miriam Buether**
Lighting **Peter Mumford**
Sound **Gareth Fry**
Choreographer **Leon Baugh**
Boxing Trainer **Errol Christie**
Casting Directors **Amy Ball & Julia Horan**
Production Manager **Paul Handley**
Stage Manager **Ben Delfont**
Deputy Stage Manager **Tamara Albachari**
Assistant Stage Manager **Lindsey Knight**
Costume Supervisor **Jackie Orton**
Dialect Coach **Majella Hurley**
Stage Management Work Placement **Kimberley Brewin**
Set & Auditorium **Weld-Fab Stage Engineering Ltd, Object Construction**

The Royal Court and Stage Management also wish to thank the follwing for their help with this production: Paul Batty and Oscar Baldry at Price & Meyers, Gymbox, Repton Boxing Club, Vertigo Rigging Ltd.

With special thanks to Hofesh Shechter for Research and Development work.

THE COMPANY

ROY WILLIAMS (Writer)

FOR THE ROYAL COURT: Fallout, Clubland, Lift Off.

OTHER THEATRE INCLUDES: Category B, Starstruck (Tricycle); Out of the Fog (Almeida); Joe Guy (Titata Fahodzi/Soho); Absolute Beginners (Lyric Theatre Hammersmith); Sing Yer Heart Out for the Lads, Baby Girl, Slow Time (National); Josie's Boys (Red Ladder); Night & Day (Theatre Venture); Angel House, Little Sweet Thing (Eclipse Theatre Tour); There's Only One Wayne Matthews (Polka); Days of Significance (RSC); Souls (Theatre Centre); The Gift (Birmingham Rep); Local Boy (Hampstead); No Boys Cricket Club (Theatre Royal Stratford East).

TELEVISION INCLUDES: Offside, Babyfather, Fallout, Ten Minute Tale.

RADIO INCLUDES: Homeboys, Tell Tale, To Sir with Love, Westway, Choice of Straws.

AWARDS INCLUDE: 31st John Whiting Award, 1997 Alfred Fagon Award, 1998 EMMA Award for Starstruck. 2000 George Devine Award for Lift Off. 2001 Evening Standard Charles Wintour Award for most Promising Playwright for Clubland. 2004 South Bank Show Arts Council Decibel Award for Fallout. 2002 BAFTA Award, for Best Children's Drama for Offside. 2008 Screen Nation Award for achievement in screenwriting for Fallout. Awarded an OBE by Her Majesty the Queen for services to Drama in 2008.

LEON BAUGH (Choreographer)

DANCE INCLUDES: (as Senior Dancer & Deputy Rehearsal Director) In Your Rooms, Uprising (Hofesh Shechter Company/Sadlers Wells/Jacobs Pillow Festival/New York City Centre). Other dance includes work for Jasmin Vardimon, Stan Won't Dance, and Frantic Assembly. Leon also played the Walrus in Pina Bausch's Masurca Fogo at Sadlers Wells.

TV INCLUDES: (as Assistant Choreographer) Skins.

GARY BEADLE (Ray)

FOR THE ROYAL COURT: God's Second in Command

OTHER THEATRE INCLUDES: Family Man, Alterations (Theatre Royal Stratford East); Top Dog Under Dog (Sheffield Crucible); The Memory of Water (Watford Palace Theatre); Generations of the Dead in the Abyss of Coney Island Madness (Contact Theatre); Ticker Tape and V Signs (7:84 Theatre Co); Welcome Home Jacko (Black Theatre Co-op/New York); Moby Dick (Royal Exchange Manchester); Club Mix (Riverside Studios).

TELEVISION INCLUDES: Casualty, Doctors, The Sarah Jane Adventures, Thieves Are Us, Kerrching, Little Britain, Holby City, Eastenders, Family Affairs, The Bill, Operation Good Guy, Born to Run, Thieftakers, Glam Metal Detectives, Shall I Be Mother?, Saturday Action, Murphy's Mob, The Lenny Henry Show, Relative Strangers, Absolutely Fabulous, Honeymoon Just Like Mohicans, Club Mix, Big Mix, Radical Chambers, Soap 18 – 30, Q.P.R. Askey Is Dead, G.L.C., Spaghetti Hoops, Les Dogs, I Love Keith Allen, Screenplay, Making Out, Jealousy, The Crying Game, Wail Of The Banshee, Space Virgins from Planet Sex, Queen of the Wild Frontier, Detectives on the Edge of a Nervous Breakdown, The Detectives, Paparazzo.

FILM INCLUDES: Til Death Do Us Part, Wit, The Imitators, Driven, Memoirs of a Survivor, Fords on Water, Absolute Beginners, Playing Away, Cresta Run, White Mischief, Malice in Wonderland.

BOXING: Schoolboy Amateur.

Gary is also Fight Captain for this production.

MIRIAM BUETHER (Designer)

FOR THE ROYAL COURT: Cock, Relocated, My Child, The Wonderful World of Dissocia (National Theatre of Scotland Tour), Way to Heaven.

OTHER THEATRE INCLUDES: Judgement Day, When the Rain Stops Falling (Almeida); Everybody Loves a Winner (Manchester International Festival); In the Red and Brown Water, The Good Soul of Szechuan, generations, The Bee, Red Demon (Young Vic); Six Characters in Search of an Author (Chichester/ West End); The Bacchae, Realism (National Theatre of Scotland/EIF); Dalston Songs (ROH); Guantanamo Honor Bound to Defend Freedom (Tricycle/ West End/New York/San Francisco); The Bee (Soho, Japan); Long Time Dead, pool (no water) (Theatre Royal Plymouth); Trade (RSC at Soho); Platform (ICA); Bintou (Arcola).

DANCE INCLUDES: Body of Poetry (Komische Oper Berlin); Frame of View (Didy Veldman, NY); Hartstocht (Introdans, Netherlands); Possibly Six, Tenderhooks (Canadian National Ballet).

OPERA INCLUDES: Turandot (ENO); The Sacrifice (costumes only, WNO); The Death of Klinghoffer (EIF/ Scottish Opera).

AWARDS INCLUDE: 1999 Linbury Prize for Stage Design; 2004/5 Critics Award for Theatre in Scotland; 2008 The Hospital Club Creative Award for Theatre.

ERROL CHRISTIE (Boxing Trainer)

Errol is a former professional boxer and was a record-breaking amateur. In 1980 he was made captain of the England boxing team and in 1983 he became European champion. He has since built a career as a trainer and is one of the country's leading coaches of 'white-collar boxing', with students including Dermot O'Leary and Gianluca Vialli. He also works in inner-city schools, using boxing and his first-hand experiences of racism and street violence to campaign against knife and gun crime.

GARETH FRY (Sound Designer)

FOR THE ROYAL COURT: The City, O Go My Man (with Out of Joint); Talking to Terrorists (with Out of Joint); Harvest, Forty Winks, Under the Whaleback, Night Songs, Face to the Wall, Redundant, Mountain Language/Ashes to Ashes, The Country.

OTHER THEATRE INCLUDES: Endgame, Shunkin, Noise of Time (Complicité); Peter Pan, Be Near Me, Black Watch (National Theatre of Scotland); Othello (Frantic Assembly); Babel (Stan Won't Dance); Dancing at Lughnasa (Old Vic); Joe Turner's Come and Gone, Sweet Nothings, How Much is Your Iron?, The Jewish Wife (Young Vic); Macbeth (Out of Joint); The Fahrenheit Twins (Told By An Idiot); Astronaut (Theatre O); Tangle, Zero Degrees and Drifting (Unlimited); Romans in Britain, Shadowmouth (Sheffield Crucible); The Bull, The Flowerbed, Giselle (Fabulous Beast Dance/Barbican); Living Costs (DV8); The Watery Part of the World (Sound and Fury); The Cat in the Hat, Pains of Youth, Women of Troy; A Matter Of Life and Death, Attempts on her Life, Waves, Theatre of Blood, Fix Up, Iphigenia at Aulis, The Three Sisters, Ivanov, The Oresteia (National); The Overwhelming (National/New York).

RADIO INCLUDES: Jump, OK Computer, The Overwhelming.

AWARDS INCLUDE: 2007 Best Sound Design Olivier Award for Waves, 2009 Olivier Award for Black Watch.

DANIEL KALUUYA (Leon)

FOR THE ROYAL COURT: Oxford Street.

OTHER THEATRE INCLUDES: Manner of the Wicked, 5 Card Deck, Stuff I Buried in a Small Town, Doors Don't Grow on Trees (Heat & Light at Hampstead); No Entry (King's Head).

TELEVISION INCLUDES: Happy Finish, Comedy Shuffle, Doctor Who, FM, Psychoville, Lewis, Mitchell & Webb Show, Delta Forever, Silent Witness, Skins, Whistleblowers, Bellamy's People, Harry and Paul, Not Safe for Work.

FILM INCLUDES: Three Kings (short), Chatroom, Cass, Shoot the Messenger, Baby (short).

RADIO INCLUDES: BBC Blast Music- Presenter Competition, Cap-a-Britain, Sneakiepeeks.

TREVOR LAIRD (Squid)

THEATRE INCLUDES: England People Very Nice, A Statement of Regret, Mysteries (National); Foxes, Sunset and Glories, Revenger's Tragedy, Safe in Our Hands (West Yorkshire Playhouse); Master Harold and the Boys (Liverpool Everyman); You Don't Kiss (Stratford Circus); Death of a Salesman (Leicester Haymarket); An Enchanted Land (Riverside Studios); Welcome Home Jacko, Mama Dragon (& founder: Black Theatre Co-op); Strange Fruit (Sheffield Crucible); Twilight Zone, The Stranger, Moon on a Rainbow Shawl (Almeida); Colors, You Can't Take It With You (Abbey, Dublin); SUS (Portrait Theatre); The Shoemaker's Holiday (Leeds Playhouse); A Midsummer Night's Dream, Twelfth Night (Open Air Theatre, Regents Park); Othello (Trivoli Theatre, Dublin/Japan); Much Ado About Nothing (Oxford Stage Company); Seafarers (Live Theatre); Song Of An Honorary Soulman (Smilin' Mongoose Theatre Co.).

TELEVISION INCLUDES: Sleepyhead, Waking the Dead, Dr Who, The Eagle, Peep Show, Murder Room, The Last Detective, Doctors, William & Mary, NCS Manhunt, Casualty, Undercover Heart, Way Out Of Order, The New Statesman, Crown Court, Struggle, Grange Hill, Bernard and the Genie, The Lenny Henry Show, Holby City, Call Me Mister, Give Us A Break, Big Deal, Dear Heart, Easy Money, Pocket Full Of Dreams, Maybury, Waterloo Sunset, Vanishing Army, Victims Of Apartheid, Playthings.

FILM INCLUDES: Hope & Glory, Love, Honour & Obey, Secrets & Lies, Smack &Thistle, Billy The Kid, The Green Baize, The Flying Devils, Slipstream, My Ticket for the Titanic, Water, Babylon, The Long Good Friday, Quadrophenia.

NIGEL LINDSAY (Charlie)

FOR THE ROYAL COURT: The Woman Before, Push Up, King Lear.

OTHER THEATRE INCLUDES: Under the Blue Sky (Duke of York's, West End); The Homecoming, Awake & Sing, Romance, The Earthly Paradise, The Tower (Almeida); Guys & Dolls (Piccadilly Theatre, West End); The Pillowman (National); The Tempest (Old Vic); Bedroom Farce (Aldwych, West End); The Real Thing (Donmar/Albery, West End/Broadway); Morphic Resonance (Donmar); London Cuckolds, Blue Remembered Hills (National); Dealer's Choice (National/Vaudeville, West End); World Music, Hamlet (Sheffield Crucible);; Katerina (Lyric Hammersmith); Relative Values (Salisbury Playhouse); Anna Karenina (Shared Experience).

TELEVISION INCLUDES: Spooks, Silent Witness, Waking the Dead, The Relief of Belsen, Rome, Jam & Jerusalem, OK Corral, All About George, New Tricks, Tunnel of Love, Frances Tuesday, Murphy's Law, My Family, I'm Alan Partridge, Midsomer Murders, The Armando Iannucci Show, Too Much Sun, Déjà vu, A Dance to the Music of Time, Harbour Lights, Bye Bye Baby, Brass Eye, Dressing for Breakfast, A Few Short Journeys of the Heart, Between the Lines.

FILM INCLUDES: Sizzle, Four Lions, Scoop, On a Clear Day, Blackball, Mike Bassett: England Manager, Rogue Trader.

RADIO INCLUDES: Alex Tripped on my Fairy, Number 10, A Pin to see the Peepshow, Lucky Numbers, The Face of the Enemy, House of Milton Jones, Frederick & Augusta, Morphic Resonance, People Like Us, Crossing the Equator.

JASON MAZA (Tommy)

THEATRE INCLUDES: Mad Blud, No Gypsy Child of Mine (Theatre Royal Stratford); Flight Path (Bush); The Cage (Nuffield Theatre); Gutted (Tristan Bates).

TELEVISION INCLUDES: Whitechapel, The Unsinkable Titanic, A Touch of Frost, Trial & Retribution.

FILM INCLUDES: Fish Tank, Ten Dead Men, Shifty, Rise of the Footsoldier, Fit, Special People, Life & Lyrics, The Tapes, Kick-Off.

PETER MUMFORD (Lighting Designer)

FOR THE ROYAL COURT: Cock, The Seagull, Dying City (& set).

OTHER THEATRE INCLUDES: The Misanthrope, Prick Up Your Ears (Comedy); A Midsummer Night's Dream, Bedroom Farce, Miss Julie (The Rose); A View from the Bridge (Duke of York's); Pictures from an Exhibition (Young Vic); Parlour Song, Cloud Nine, Hedda Gabler, The Goat (Almeida); All's Well That Ends Well (National); Carousel, Fiddler on the Roof (Savoy); Hamlet, Brand, Macbeth (RSC); Private Lives (West End/Broadway).

OPERA & DANCE INCLUDES: E=mc2 (Birmingham Royal Ballet); Elegy for Young Lovers (ENO at The Young Vic); Petrushka, Carmen (also set), Cheating, Lying, Stealing (Scottish Ballet); Prima Donna (Manchester International Festival); La Cenerentola (Glyndebourne); Bluebeard's Castle, Madame Butterfly, Così fan tutte, Die Soldaten, Poppea (ENO); Il Trovatore (Paris); La Traviata (Antwerp); Siegfried, Götterdämmerung, Fidelio, Don Giovanni (Scottish Opera); Madama Butterfly (Opera North); Giulio Cesare (Bordeaux); Madame Butterfly, Peter Grimes, 125th Gala (Metropolitan Opera, NYC); Eugene Onegin, The Bartered Bride (ROH); Earth & the Great Weather (also directed) (Almeida Opera); L'Heure Espagnole, L'Enfant et les Sortilèges (Opera Zuid).

TELEVISION INCLUDES: 48 Preludes & Fugues, Mathew Bourne's Swan Lake.

AWARDS INCLUDE: 1995 Olivier Award for Outstanding Achievement in Dance for The Glass Blew In (Siobhan Davies) and Fearful Symmetries (Royal Ballet), 2003 Best Lighting Olivier Award for Bacchai (National).

SARAH RIDGEWAY (Becky)

THEATRE INCLUDES: Days of Significance (RSC); Comedy of Errors (Shakespeare's Globe); A Taste of Honey (Salisbury Playhouse); Romeo & Juliet (Northern Broadsides); Write Now Festival (Manchester Royal Exchange).

TELEVISION INCLUDES: Doctors, Miss Marple, The Bill, Eastenders, The Worst Witch, Jonathan Creek.

FILM INCLUDES: 14, Memorablis.

SACHA WARES (Director)

FOR THE ROYAL COURT: random (& Theatre Local/Tour), My Child, Credible Witness.

OTHER THEATRE INCLUDES: generations (Young Vic); trade (RSC/Soho); Platform (ICA); A Number (Theatre Project Tokyo); Guantanamo (co-directed with Nicolas Kent, Tricycle/West End/New York); Bintou (Arcola); Six Degrees of Separation (Sheffield Crucible); Pera Palas (NT Springboards at The Gate); One Life and Counting (Bush).

Sacha is Associate Director at the Royal Court.

ANTHONY WELSH (Troy)

THEATRE INCLUDES: Pornography (Tricycle); Brothers Size (Young Vic).

TELEVISION INCLUDES: The Bill.

FILM INCLUDES: Red Tails.

THE ENGLISH STAGE COMPANY
AT THE ROYAL COURT THEATRE

'For me the theatre is really a religion or way of life. You must decide what you feel the world is about and what you want to say about it, so that everything in the theatre you work in is saying the same thing ... A theatre must have a recognisable attitude. It will have one, whether you like it or not.'

George Devine, first artistic director of the English Stage Company: notes for an unwritten book.

photo: Stephen Cummiskey

As Britain's leading national company dedicated to new work, the Royal Court Theatre produces new plays of the highest quality, working with writers from all backgrounds, and addressing the problems and possibilities of our time.

"The Royal Court has been at the centre of British cultural life for the past 50 years, an engine room for new writing and constantly transforming the theatrical culture." Stephen Daldry

Since its foundation in 1956, the Royal Court has presented premieres by almost every leading contemporary British playwright, from John Osborne's Look Back in Anger to Caryl Churchill's A Number and Tom Stoppard's Rock 'n' Roll. Just some of the other writers to have chosen the Royal Court to premiere their work include Edward Albee, John Arden, Richard Bean, Samuel Beckett, Edward Bond, Leo Butler, Jez Butterworth, Martin Crimp, Ariel Dorfman, Stella Feehily, Christopher Hampton, David Hare, Eugène Ionesco, Ann Jellicoe, Terry Johnson, Sarah Kane, David Mamet, Martin McDonagh, Conor McPherson, Joe Penhall, Lucy Prebble, Mark Ravenhill, Simon Stephens, Wole Soyinka, Polly Stenham, David Storey, Debbie Tucker Green, Arnold Wesker and Roy Williams.

"It is risky to miss a production there." Financial Times

In addition to its full-scale productions, the Royal Court also facilitates international work at a grass roots level, developing exchanges which bring young writers to Britain and sending British writers, actors and directors to work with artists around the world. The research and play development arm of the Royal Court Theatre, The Studio, finds the most exciting and diverse range of new voices in the UK. The Studio runs play-writing groups including the Young Writers Programme, Critical Mass for black, Asian and minority ethnic writers and the biennial Young Writers Festival. For further information, go to www.royalcourttheatre.com/ywp.

"Yes, the Royal Court is on a roll. Yes, Dominic Cooke has just the genius and kick that this venue needs… It's fist-bitingly exciting." Independent

Supported by
ARTS COUNCIL ENGLAND

PROGRAMME SUPPORTERS

The Royal Court (English Stage Company Ltd) receives its principal funding from Arts Council England, London. It is also supported financially by a wide range of private companies, charitable and public bodies, and earns the remainder of its income from the box office and its own trading activities.

The Genesis Foundation supports the Royal Court's work with International Playwrights. Theatre Local is sponsored by Bloomberg. The Jerwood Charitable Foundation supports new plays by new playwrights through the Jerwood New Playwrights series.

The Artistic Director's Chair is supported by a lead grant from The Peter Jay Sharp Foundation, contributing to the activities of the Artistic Director's office. Over the past ten years the BBC has supported the Gerald Chapman Fund for directors.

ROYAL COURT DEVELOPMENT ADVOCATES
John Ayton
Elizabeth Bandeen
Tim Blythe
Anthony Burton
Sindy Caplan
Cas Donald (Vice Chair)
Allie Esiri
Celeste Fenichel
Anoushka Healy
Stephen Marquardt
Emma Marsh (Chair)
Mark Robinson
William Russell
Deborah Shaw Marquardt (Vice Chair)
Nick Wheeler
Daniel Winterfeldt

PUBLIC FUNDING
Arts Council England, London
British Council

CHARITABLE DONATIONS
American Friends of the Royal Court Theatre
Anthony Burton
The Brim Foundation*
Gerald Chapman Fund
Columbia Foundation
Cowley Charitable Trust
The Edmond de Rothschild Foundation*
The Epstein Parton Foundation*
Do Well Foundation Ltd*
The Eranda Foundation
Frederick Loewe Foundation*
Genesis Foundation
The Golden Bottle Trust
The Goldsmiths' Company
The H & G de Freitas Charitable Trust
Jerwood Charitable Foundation
John Thaw Foundation
John Lyon's Charity
J Paul Getty Jnr Charitable Trust
The Laura Pels Foundation*
Marina Kleinwort Trust
The Martin Bowley Charitable Trust
The Andrew W. Mellon Foundation
Paul Hamlyn Foundation
Jerome Robbins Foundation*

Rose Foundation
Rosenkranz Foundation
The Peter Jay Sharp Foundation*

CORPORATE SUPPORTERS & SPONSORS
BBC
Bloomberg
Coutts & Co
Ecosse Films
French Wines
Grey London
Gymbox
Kudos Film & Television
Moët & Chandon

BUSINESS ASSOCIATES, MEMBERS & BENEFACTORS
Auerbach & Steele Opticians
Hugo Boss
Lazard
Bank of America Merrill Lynch
Vanity Fair

AMERICAN FRIENDS OF THE ROYAL COURT
Rachel Bail
Francis Finlay
Amanda Foreman & Jonathan Barton
Imelda Liddiard
Stephen McGruder & Angeline Goreau
Alexandra Munroe & Robert Rosenkranz
Ben Rauch & Margaret Scott
David & Andrea Thurm
Amanda Vaill & Tom Stewart
Monica Voldstad
Franklin Wallis

INDIVIDUAL MEMBERS
ICE-BREAKERS
Act IV
Anonymous
Rosemary Alexander
Ossi & Paul Burger
Mrs Helena Butler
Lindsey Carlon
Mark & Tobey Dichter
Virginia Finegold
Charlotte & Nick Fraser
Sebastian & Rachel Grigg
David Lanch
Colette & Peter Levy
Larry & Peggy Levy
Watcyn Lewis
Mr & Mrs Peter Lord
David Marks QC

Nicola McFarland
Janet & Michael Orr
Pauline Pinder
Mr & Mrs William Poeton
The Really Useful Group
Lois Sieff OBE
Nick & Louise Steidl
Laura & Stephen Zimmerman

GROUND-BREAKERS
Anonymous
Moira Andreae
Jane Attias*
Elizabeth & Adam Bandeen
Dr Kate Best
Philip Blackwell
Stan & Val Bond
Mrs D H Brett
Sindy & Jonathan Caplan
Mr & Mrs Gavin Casey
Tim & Caroline Clark
Kay Ellen Consolver
Clyde Cooper
Ian & Caroline Cormack
Mr & Mrs Cross
Andrew & Amanda Cryer
Rob & Cherry Dickins
Denise & Randolph Dumas
Robyn M Durie
Allie Esiri
Celeste & Peter Fenichel
Margy Fenwick
Edwin Fox Foundation
John Garfield
Beverley Gee
Nick & Julie Gould
Lord & Lady Grabiner
Richard & Marcia Grand*
Nick Gray
Reade & Elizabeth Griffith
Don & Sue Guiney
Jill Hackel & Andrzej Zarzycki
Douglas & Mary Hampson
Sam & Caroline Haubold
Anoushka Healy
Mr & Mrs J Hewett
The David Hyman Charitable Trust
David P Kaskel & Christopher A Teano
Peter & Maria Kellner*
Steve Kingshott
Mrs Joan Kingsley & Mr Philip Kingsley
Mr & Mrs Pawel Kisielewski
Kathryn Ludlow
Emma Marsh
David & Elizabeth Miles
Barbara Minto

The North Street Trust
Gavin & Ann Neath
Murray North
Clive & Annie Norton
William Plapinger & Cassie Murray*
Wendy & Philip Press
Serena Prest
Mr & Mrs Tim Reid
Paul & Gill Robinson
Paul & Jill Ruddock
William & Hilary Russell
Julie & Bill Ryan
Sally & Anthony Salz
The Michael & Melanie Sherwood Foundation
Anthony Simpson & Susan Boster
Brian D Smith
Samantha & Darren Smith
Sheila Steinberg
Carl & Martha Tack
The Ury Trust
Edgar & Judith Wallner
Nick & Chrissie Wheeler
Sian & Matthew Westerman
Katherine & Michael Yates*

BOUNDARY-BREAKERS
Katie Bradford
Tim Fosberry
Lydia & Manfred Gorvy

MOVER-SHAKERS
Anonymous
John and Annoushka Ayton
Cas & Philip Donald
Lloyd & Sarah Dorfman
Duncan Matthews QC
The David & Elaine Potter Charitable Foundation
Ian & Carol Sellars
Jan & Michael Topham

HISTORY-MAKERS
Jack & Linda Keenan*
Miles Morland

MAJOR DONORS
Rob & Siri Cope
Daniel & Joanna Friel
Deborah & Stephen Marquardt
Lady Sainsbury of Turville
NoraLee & Jon Sedmak*
The Williams Charitable Trust

*Supporters of the American Friends of the Royal Court (AFRCT)

Sucker Punch

Characters

Leon, *black, 16–20*
Troy, *black, 16–20*
Becky, *white, 16–20*
Charlie, *white, 46–50*
Tommy, *white, 20–24*
Ray, *black, 35*
Squid, *black, 40–44*

Act One

Gym.

Charlie *is doing pad work with* **Tommy**.

Charlie Jab. Double jab, cross. Jab, hook to body. One, two, three, four, stepping forward jab and again. Hook, slip. And again. Come on, double jab. Cross, hook, uppercut. Uppercut. Jab. Sit down. Sit down. Hook, uppercut, uppercut. Slip. Sit down. Sit down. Jab. Sit down. Sit down. One, two. One, two. One, two, three, four, double jab. Cross, hook, uppercut, uppercut, Sit down. Cross, sit down. Slip. Slip, slip, slip, slip, slip, slip, slip, slip, slip. On yer jab, sit down.

Leon *and* **Troy** *come in arguing.*

Troy Yer a one little batty bwoi and a half, Leon.

Leon Cry all you like, Troy, I ain't doing it.

Charlie One, two.

Troy Neither am I, dread.

Leon We flipped the coin. Heads I mop the floor, tails you clean the bogs. Fair's fair, Troy boy, I won.

Troy How was I supposed to know what you were flipping the coin for?

Leon Then why call it for, dopey?

Troy Have you seen the amount of shit that are in those bowls? It's just wrong.

Leon (*aside*) That's white boys for you.

Troy Nasty.

Leon (*giggles*) Best get to it. Chop-chop.

Troy I ain't going in there again.

Leon   I know I'm not.

Troy   Flip again? Use my coin.

Leon   Move yerself.

Troy   Then I'll help you with the floor, you help me in the bogs.

Leon   No, I'm alright, man.

Troy   Oh come on, Leon.

Leon   Toilets are waiting, Troy.

Charlie   Jab, slip, hook.

Troy   It's your bloody fault we are here in the first place.

Leon   You wanna run that by me again?

Troy   I told you to keep a lookout.

Leon   I told you not to break in.

Troy   If you had done yer job.

Leon   Here we go.

Troy   We woulda got away.

Leon   Every time, man.

Troy   Just pass me that mop.

Leon   No.

Troy   Pass me the mop.

Leon   Come get it.

Troy   Don't make me hurt you.

Leon   Oh yes?

Troy   You facety little rass.

Charlie   Oi, Lenny Henry! Shut it.

Leon   Oh shame.

Troy   Chip!

Leon   Take the blame!

Charlie   You as well, Leon.

Leon   Me?

Troy   What was that about taking the shame?

Charlie   How's that shoulder? Still a bit stiff?

Tommy   Like a motherfucker.

Charlie   Like a what?

Tommy   Don't blame me, it's them. (*Points to* **Leon** *and* **Troy**.) The way they talk, is like a disease.

Troy   What this rass just say about us?

Charlie   Troy, back off right now.

Troy   I want my five pounds back.

Leon   Say again?

Troy   Fiver I lent you yesterday. I want it back.

Leon   Don't have it.

Troy   You lie.

Leon   I spent it.

Troy   On what?

Leon   What are you, Babylon?

Troy   Yer give it to yer dad?

Leon   Look, I spent it, it's gone, you can't have it back.

Troy   Alright, don't cry.

Leon   I'm not.

Charlie (*snaps*)   Don't let me tell you two again, now shut it.

Leon Every time I'm with you, I always get it in the neck.

Troy Mop?

Leon Yer not having it.

Charlie Come on, Tommy, speed up, move your feet. How many more times?

Tommy *goes faster.*

Charlie Alright, Alright. That's enough. You're just not with it today.

Tommy Hold up, give us a chance.

Charlie I've seen snails go faster.

Tommy Bloody hell, Chas.

Charlie Shower, now.

Tommy *gets out of the ring and heads for the shower.*

Charlie (*notices* **Leon** *and* **Troy**) Isn't one of you supposed to be doing the bogs right now?

Leon/Troy (*both pointing at the other*) Him!

Charlie Why don't we try again?

Troy Bin telling him, Chas.

Leon And I've been telling him.

Charlie Decide now, the pair of you, or you'll both be doing it. I want those toilet seats looking like mirrors.

Troy How long are you going to keep punishing us?

Charlie Oh, what's the matter, Troy, scared of a little bit of hard work. (*Chuckles.*) Take that up with your mum.

Charlie *goes into his office.* **Troy** *kicks over a nearby bucket in anger.*

Leon Why don't you just chill out for once?

Troy I want my fiver.

Leon   Troy, I need it.

Troy   Thought you said you spent it.

Leon   I will. Soon as she says yes.

Troy   Who?

Leon   Beverley Arnett of course.

Troy   Beverley Arnett from Edward Woods Estate?

Leon   You know any other Beverley Arnetts from Edward Woods Estate? Wanna take her to see *Airplane*.

Troy   You ain't got a chance, man.

Leon   Say again?

Troy   Clean out your ears, ain't got a chance, boy.

Leon   Rewind your brain back to last week, Troy, you said you know her, you said you put a word in for me.

Troy   I know, I did.

Leon   So?

Troy   There was little complication.

Leon   What little complication?

Troy   She don't wanna know.

Leon   What you mean she don't wanna know?

Troy   Alright, don't get vex.

Leon   What did you say to her?

Troy   I told her what you look like.

Leon   What?

Troy   She weren't going for it, sorry.

Leon   Don't tell her what I look like.

Troy   She wanted to know.

Leon I bet you said I had rubber lips and dried-up hands.

Troy Leon, I am hurt. I really am. Not once did I ever say that you had dried-up hands.

Leon Bastard man. Think yer all sweetness and light wid gal.

Troy Just like coffee, Leon, ca I grind so fine! You are better off with that African one who's always following you around at school.

Leon (*disgusted*) Yinka!

Troy (*bad African accent*) Leon, I love you!

Leon Oh, you're definitely cruising for it now, brown sugar.

Troy Come and have a go, Black Mariah.

Leon Gladly!

The boys spar around the gym, laughing. They are clearly enjoying each other's company. **Becky**, **Charlie**'s *daughter, enters. The boys stop playing and are eyeing her up.*

Troy Oh yes, and today's lucky lady is this fine redhead, sitting over there. She like a Page Three girl but without the tittie, innit?

Leon That's Charlie's little girl – you want to mess around with that?

Troy Never tell Troy what he cannot do, because all he is going to think of is how to do it.

Leon She goes to that posh school, Lady Margaret's.

Troy And?

Leon She's on my bus.

Troy Still waiting?

Leon I've seen half a dozen boys try and get to her. She went all Blankety Blank on them.

Troy Yeah, but they were nothing but boys though.

Leon   Listen to him.

Troy   And learn.

Troy *approaches* **Becky**.

Troy   Excuse me, sorry to bother you, but do your legs hurt?

Becky   No.

Troy   Are you sure?

Becky   Why?

Troy   Cos you've been running through my head ever since I saw you.

Becky (*giggles*)   No thanks, Troy.

Troy   You know my name?

Becky   Course I know your name. You're the one who broke in here a few weeks back. You and him. I thought my dad was going to kill you. Are you trying to look down my shirt?

Troy   I was trying to read the label.

Becky   What label?

Troy   The one that says 'Made in Heaven'.

Becky (*chuckles*)   You lot. You really love yourselves don't yer?

Troy   You mean black lot?

Becky   What do you think my dad would do to you if he saw you talking to me right now?

Tommy (*coming back from the shower*)   Turn him white, that's what.

Troy   Yeah, you keep going with that mouth of yours, Tommy. Hey, baby, I hope you're not going on my account.

Becky   Talk is cheap and so are you.

Tommy (*to* **Troy**)   Don't you have toilets to clean or summin, boy?

Troy   Alright, now did he just call me boy now?

Leon   Troy?

Troy   No, but this *boomba* is asking for it, Leon, seriously.

Leon   Just forget it.

All the boys jump and panic when **Charlie** *comes out of his office.*

Charlie   I'm hearing a lot of chatter going out here. That can only mean one thing.

Leon   Mopping the floor, Mr Maggs!

Tommy   On my way out, Chas.

Charlie   And you?

Troy   Toilets, I know . . .

Charlie   Don't let me keep you. (*Sees* **Becky**.) Becky, what you doing here? You know the rules, darling.

Becky   I wouldn't be here if I wasn't locked out. Keys, Dad?

Charlie *throws her his keys.*

Charlie   Now, home.

Charlie *goes back in his office.*

Becky   Just get 'em cut.

Troy   Laters, Becky.

Becky   See you, Leon.

Becky *goes.* **Troy** *scoffs.*

Troy   What de rah? In all my days, I've never seen a girl bypass me in order to reach a rubber lips.

Leon   Say what?

Troy   Gal called yer name Leon, she is up for it.

Leon   She have good taste.

Tommy   Fancy your chances, Leon?

Troy   What if?

Tommy   You lot are so busy throwing petrol bombs, you wouldn't know what to do with a woman.

Troy   Rass!

Tommy   Watched some of your boys going mad again last night.

Troy   Oh, hear him now.

Tommy   Tearing up Brixton they were, what's that about?

Troy   Batty bwoi police throwing their weight about again, that's what.

Tommy   What have they been putting in your water, eh?

Troy   Tommy getting fresh now!

Leon   Better believe.

Troy   He had better just chip. Or he be MIA like that, cha rass.

Tommy   Get a job, the lot of yer.

Troy   You know, it's funny how I don't see you looking yer nose down at the black man when you get the shakes for a little bit of spliff, *Thomas*!

Tommy   Oi!

Troy   I see you on the estate, following them Rastas about, begging them for a lickle squeeze.

Tommy   Keep yer voice down, will yer?

Troy   Why is that?

Leon   Cos Charlie will kick his arse to the Bridge and back again, that's why.

Troy   That true, Tommy?

Tommy   Come on, Troy, you know I don't mean anything by it. I'm just messing wid yer, thass all. (*Puts on patois.*) *Ease up nuh, man!*

Troy   Hear him, Leon?

Leon   Loud and clear, Troy.

Tommy   *Watcha talking about, Willis?*

Troy   In all my days.

Tommy (*puts out his hand*)   Gimme five!

Troy   Never hear a dog beg so.

Tommy   Fuck yer then!

Troy   I'd fuck yer mum, dread. But she so ugly, she makes onions cry.

Tommy   And yours only wears knickers to keep her ankles warm.

Leon   Oh!

Troy *is in a rage. He goes for* **Tommy** *but* **Leon** *grabs him.*

Leon   Troy, don't, man.

Troy   You hear that?

Leon   If we fuck up again, Mr Maggs will throw our arses out.

Troy   I don't business about that.

Leon   And tell the police what we did. Ease up.

Leon *sees* **Tommy** *smirking.*

Leon   You know, I'd wipe off that smile if I were you.

Tommy   What, he can slag off my mum, but I can't slag off his?

Leon   Yeah, that's right.

Tommy   Jog on, boy.

Leon   You wanna die today?

Tommy   You think you've the shoes to take me on as well, do yer, Leon? Let's see what you've got.

Leon   Leave me.

Tommy *jabs at* **Leon**.

Leon   I'll hurt ya.

Tommy *clips him on the cheek.*

Leon   I mean it.

Troy   Leon?

Tommy *clips him again.*

Leon   I'll do it.

Tommy   I'm hearing a lot of barks here.

Troy   Slap him.

Leon *tries to take a swing at him but misses.*

Tommy   Do you wanna try that again?

Leon *tries hard to jab* **Tommy**. *They both circle around each other.*

Charlie *comes out of his office. He is about to say something but chooses to watch what happens instead.*

Tommy   Come on then.

Leon   I'm coming.

Tommy   Can't you take it?

Leon *clips* **Tommy** *on the face.*

Troy   Oh!

Leon   Yes! I got yer!

Troy   Under manners!

Tommy   Yeah, yeah!

Leon   I got you.

Tommy   Every dog has its day, Leon.

Leon   I got you!

Tommy   Think yer the dogs now?

Leon   I don't think.

Charlie   So, what is all this then?

Tommy   These two again, Chas.

Leon   You grass and a half.

Charlie   I don't want to hear a word out of you. Unless you want the Old Bill breathing down. Floor!

Leon *returns to mopping up*.

Charlie (*sees* **Troy** *glaring*)   You got something to say?

Tommy   Running round here like monkeys, doing all sorts.

Troy   Wass he saying now?

Leon   Back off, Troy.

Charlie   I'll have coppers here in five, so help me God, Troy, now clean!

Leon *and* **Troy** *back away*.

Charlie   Now was it me or did that little *monkey* just gave you a right slap just now.

Tommy   He was lucky.

Charlie   If you were any good or half as fast, he would never have got that close. You're fighting for the ABA title soon, what's the matter wid yer? Yer getting slow, boy.

Tommy   Don't talk to me like that in front of them.

Charlie   Oi, you're the one he got.

Tommy   You're the one who's going soft. Shoulda set the Old Bill on them.

Charlie   I think you had better get yer arse home right bloody now. Yer head ain't right.

Tommy *storms off.*

Charlie   Don't come back until you start using it.

Troy   Heads or tails?

Leon   Troy, I'm not doing it.

Charlie (*to* **Leon**)   Where you going?

Leon   I got a floor to mop.

Charlie   Where'd you learn to fight like that?

Leon   School.

Charlie   So, you're not just some thieving little git then?

Leon   Look, we're really sorry for breaking in, Mr Maggs.

Charlie   Never mind all that.

He throws him a pair of gloves.

Get those on. (*To* **Troy**.) You, bogs! (*To* **Leon**.) Well, don't just stand there like a lemon, let's see what you've got.

Leon *addresses the audience.*

Leon   The first fight I'm having is with some tall, skinny-looking kid. From the minute I step into the ring, he's staring me out, like I burgled his house. What am I doing here . . . ? Oh! He lands one right on me. I'm going dizzy, I'm all numb. I wanna go home. I'll keep out of his way.

Bell rings.

Crowd seem to like it when I move around. I'll go a bit faster then. They're lapping it up. Let's see if they like this. Bop my shoulders, spin my arm like Sugar Ray Leonard, now they're cheering, can't get enough. Skinny white boy

don't know what to do with me! I get in a jab, and it hurts
him, my first punch as well. A bit of fancy footwork now,
I think. Crowd are loving it, I'm loving it. Another jab!
Then a sweet uppercut! Skinny kid is down like a heap!
I'm taking him out, me! My first ever fight, and I took him
out. Fucking hell! Yes! What a feeling. Starting to like this.
Next up is a fighter from Repton. Mark Saunders. Half-caste
fighter from Brick Lane. Trying to find a way in here, but
he's not having any of it. It's like he can see me coming. I go
with the footwork. He can't keep up with me. I'm tiring him
out, he's dazzled by my speed. That's it, that's it, keep him
coming, keep him coming, now, have that!

He hits out with a flurry of punches.

Oh yes! I look to Charlie, he's gotta love it!

He takes a hit.

Oh that was stupid. All I can see is gloves, fuck, get me out!
My ears are ringing, I've got pins and needles all inside, gotta
take it, gotta keep up, make it to the next round, come on!

Ref stops the fight. Bell rings.

What? What . . . what the . . . what you mean he's won? Ref?
I didn't go down! I didn't go down, I was getting back up, I
had him.

The gym.

Leon *is working on his combinations.* **Squid**, *his father, is hovering
around him.*

Squid   It was Richard Thomas.

Leon   Who?

Squid   Richard Thomas, boy.

Leon   Never heard of him.

Squid   Crazy black man, live off Hurlingham Road, you
know him, man. Always yelling, mostly to himself. You
remember, man.

Leon No, I don't.

Squid Richard. Richard Thomas, man.

Leon Yeah, keep saying his name like it's going to make a difference.

Squid Facety bwoi! He grew up in Cleveland, you played football with his nephew, Joe.

Leon Dad, for the last time, I've never heard of him.

Squid No mind.

Leon Good.

Squid Thing is, back in the day he could fight too, Oh Lord could he fight! Never lost, till that one time when he got his retina detached. He used to scare his opponents half to death by roaring like a lion at the beginning of each round, for trut! Then he just go, punch, punch and punch! None of this jab, uppercut shit, just punch! That's where you go wrong all the time.

Leon I nearly won.

Squid What you mean you nearly won? You lost.

Leon Yeah, alright!

Squid You know how much money I lose betting on you?

Leon I'm sorry.

Squid Shoulda finished him, never let it get that far.

Leon I know that. I'll win again. (*Sees* **Squid** *scorn.*) I will!

Squid Tell me summin, who's looking after yer money?

Leon What money?

Squid You have two fights and you don't earn any money? What the hell is wrong wid you?

Leon It's amateur, Dad, you don't get money.

Squid   So, you let some white boys bust you up in the ring . . .

Leon   I bust them up as well.

Squid   And you have nothing to show for it? That don't mek sense.

Leon   It does.

Squid   Hey, when chicken tie up chicken, cockroach want explanation.

Leon   What?

Squid   Just tell me you still have yer job in Wimpy.

Leon   Yeah, I still got *that*.

Squid   You get paid today, right?

Leon   And here it comes.

Squid *starts to dance.*

Leon   Dad, don't, not here.

Squid   Have to, feeling the vibe!

Leon   Not going to work. Not going to work. (*He is cracking.*) No.

Squid   *You know you wanna, you wanna . . .*

Leon   No.

Squid   Just this once.

Leon   It's always this one.

Squid   Three thirty at Kempton. Spanish Eyes. It is a sure ting.

Leon   It's always a sure *ting*. (*Trying not to look.*) You can dance till Christmas, man.

Squid   Leon?

Leon Dad, I had to buy my kit. Pay my dues. All I had left is a bit for Mum.

Squid Where it deh?

Leon She has it.

Squid Nuttin but a waste of blasted time. Showing you my finest moves like some claart!

Leon Finest?

Squid You are a facety bwoi! Disco-dance champion –

Leon – 1973!

Squid You wanna know how many babies I make that year cos of my moves? You have no idea.

Leon Who are you on with it now?

Squid What you makes think I am on with anybody?

Leon Your Brut aftershave. You stink of it. You are on the scent. I bet I know.

Squid Oh yes, bet, my favourite word. Whatever you have?

Leon Cool.

Squid Well, come on, big man.

Leon No lie?

Squid No lie! Come.

Leon Mrs Hawkins from the chemist. Curly brown hair. Always strolling around on the estate in her tight blue jeans.

Squid Nope!

Leon Get out.

Squid I say no.

Leon Dad, I've seen you, you've been moving in on her for weeks. Play fair, don't lie!

Squid   Who's lying? It is Mrs Deakin from the chemist, not Hawkins. Gimme me my money.

Leon   Same woman.

Squid   Wrong name. Mrs Hawkins works in Rumbelows, off the high street. But I wouldn't touch her wid yours.

Leon   Shit!

Squid   Always know how the cards are stack before you gamble, boy. Now gwan fetch my money.

Leon *goes to his locker. He takes out his wallet and hands* **Squid** *some notes.*

Leon   Just make sure you bet on me next time. I'm gonna knock him out, whoever he is.

Squid   Like you knock out the Saunders boy? Tell me, what was all that dancing shit you were doing?

Leon   The crowd liked it.

Squid   You look like a jackarse!

Leon   You can talk.

Squid   Oh! So boy tink him man now.

Leon   No thinking necessary.

Squid   Come nuh, guard up.

Leon   I don't feel like it.

Squid   Show me some moves.

Leon   I got training.

Squid   Come on.

Leon   Dad.

Squid   Come on.

Leon   Get off!

Squid   What yer bawling for?

Leon   I'm not.

Squid   You want yer money back?

Leon   Keep it.

Squid   If you go cry about it.

Leon   I said no.

Charlie *comes out of his office, followed by* **Becky**.

Becky   No, Dad, those ones were last year's.

Charlie   Well, I can't help you then.

Becky   You have got to keep better records than this.

Charlie   Try the bottom drawer.

Becky   I've looked in the bottom drawer. It's a mess. Receipts everywhere. Get an accountant, you tight git.

Charlie   What's the point in paying for your fancy education if I can't take advantage of it once in a while?

Becky   You don't pay, Mum does.

Charlie   And I bet she told you to say that.

Becky   Receipts?

Charlie   Top drawer, they should be there, have another look.

Becky   Sort yourself out, Dad.

Becky *goes back into the office.* **Leon** *is staring at her.*

Charlie   What you gawping at?

Leon   Nothing, just working.

Charie   So work!

Leon   Doing it.

Charlie   Weren't doing much of anything when that Saunders lad knocked you spark out.

Leon   He didn't knock me out.

Charlie   No, you just kept running into his fist for the fun of it. Gotta smarten up, boy.

Leon   Right.

Charlie   I know I'm right. You think you're going to get anywhere by loafing around? Living on handouts?

Leon   No.

Charlie   Cos Maggie is on to you, make no mistake.

Squid (*scorns*)   Oh yes, good old Maggie!

Charlie   No offence, Squid, but you know my rule about family members in the gym whilst my boys are in training.

Squid   You want tell him to stop strutting round like some batty man.

Leon   I weren't strutting.

Charlie   You weren't keeping yer guard up either.

Squid   Thass what I tell him.

Leon   No you didn't.

Squid   I forget, I'm telling you now.

Charlie   Excuse me? Squid, if you wouldn't mind.

Squid   I'm gone, I'm gone.

Squid *leaves*.

Charlie   I'm not seeing any sweat, Leon.

Leon   Don't worry, I'm down with it.

Charlie   'Down with it'? Do I look like a bro?

Leon   No.

Charlie   Good. Cos I don't want any *down with it or down with that* in my gym. Talk more better English, like me.

Leon Yes, Mr Maggs.

Charlie Don't call me that. I work for a living. It's Charlie or Chas, your choice. Now, what are you, somebody or nobody?

Leon Somebody.

Charlie Well, come on then, Let's see some sweat here!

Becky *comes back out with a handful of bills.*

Becky Dad, all of these bills are unopened.

Charlie I thought you wanted the receipts.

Becky Why haven't you paid them?

Charlie *sees that* **Leon** *has stopped again.* **Leon** *can't take his eyes off* **Becky**.

Charlie What are you doing now?

Leon Nothing, Mr Mag— Chas . . . Charlie . . .

Charlie Could stutter for England, him.

Becky Dad?

Charlie Sweat!

Leon I'm sweating!

Charlie Let me see it!

Becky This is not going away.

Charlie *grabs a pair of pads.*

Charlie Do I have to do everything around here? Get your arse in that ring.

Tommy *enters.*

Tommy Alright, Chas?

Charlie Oh, will you look at this. Now this is what I am talking about. Please put your hands together for the new

British under 18 ABA Champion, Tommy Dobson! Leon?
Come on.

Leon *claps relunctantly.*

Charlie Always give respect where it's due. Proudest night
of my life that was. This is a boy who listens to me, who
doesn't loaf around or strut around, yeah, who knows what
he wants and will sweat buckets to get it. The pride of
Britain this one. Are you listening, Leon?

Leon Hard not to.

Charlie Tommy is a winner! (*To* **Tommy**.) Here endeth the
lesson. Get your arse over here.

Tommy (*approaches*) Cheers, Chas.

Charlie You're beautiful! So, tell me. How do you feel
about turning pro now then?

Leon Chas?

Tommy I feel alright about it, yeah. I think I'm ready.

Charlie Good, cos I've got news.

Leon Chas?

Charlie Barry Palmer has been on the blower this morning.
He wants to set up a meet with you and one of his boys.

Tommy Yeah, I know.

Charlie Well, let's have it.

Leon *gives up waiting. He decides to work out on his own.*

Tommy I told him no, Chas.

Charlie Come again?

Tommy He's in deep with loan sharks. He tells his boys to
throw fights, he's known for it. We'll get a rep.

Charlie Don't believe everything you hear.

Tommy   And his purse offer was a joke.

Charlie   You discussed money with him? No wonder. Tommy, you leave that stuff to me. Don't go punching above your weight, son. It's risky turning Palmer down like that.

Tommy   What about Mickey Bishop?

Charlie   Bishop?

Tommy   He was in the crowd – that's my second fight he's seen. He's gotta be interested.

Charlie   Whoa, cool yer jets.

Tommy   See what's occurring. He's a top-notch promoter.

Charlie   Yeah, I know who he is, thank you. I've been dealing with the likes of Bishop for twenty-odd years! I know what I'm doing.

Tommy   I'm not saying you don't, but if he's watching me –

Charlie   He watches everyone, boy, no offence. Let him come to us. In the meantime, I'll call Barry, set up something. (**Tommy** *sighs*.) Don't look at me like that, Palmer's no saint but he's got a few good prospects, not as good as you, but worthy of your time, I think. I'll have words, no funny stuff. Now smile. I won't let you down. Look at me. I'm proud of you, you know that?

Tommy   Yeah, I know.

Leon   Chas, you ready for me? I'm cooling down here.

Tommy   I thought you were having his balls for missing a fight?

Charlie   That was Troy. I know they all look the same in the dark, son.

Tommy   I can't tell them apart in the day.

Charlie (*to* **Leon**)   Come on, I wanna see it dripping off yer. (*To* **Tommy**.) Tommy, let's get Barry on the phone.

Becky (*concerned*)   Dad?

Charlie   Jesus, girl, I'll pay the bills, alright?

Becky   That's not it.

Charlie   It'll have to wait. I need the office for a bit, sweetheart, man talk.

Becky   It won't take long.

Charlie   You go on in, Tommy boy.

Tommy *goes into the office.*

Charlie   Look, I know what you're going to say.

Becky   Then what are you playing at?

Charlie   Tommy is different from the others.

Becky   How different?

Charlie   I used to spar with his old man.

Becky   So?

Charlie   He's not going to leave. He's gonna be big, my girl, and he's gonna take us with him. Smile, will yer.

Becky   Oh, Dad don't build up your hopes.

Charlie   I'm not! Anything else?

Charlie *goes into the office.* **Becky** *hits a speed bag in frustration.*

Leon   You know, you should step into it.

Becky (*riled*)   Did I ask for your opinion?

Leon   You alright?

Becky   Sweet as, Leon.

Leon   Don't look it.

Becky   I don't care.

Leon   You don't have to shout.

Becky I'm not shouting.

Leon You're not quiet.

Becky Are you trying to pull me or something?

Leon No!

Becky Well, there's a first. Usually I have to beat you lot off with a stick when I go to school in the mornings. What is it with you and white girls, eh?

Leon I came over to see if you're alright.

Becky Why shouldn't I be?

Leon Fine then. Cha!

Leon *goes at it on the punchbag.*

Becky Look, it's not you, it's my dad. He gets turned right on when one of his boys turns pro. No one else exists. He always lets himself believe they are going to take him with them to a world title.

Leon Do they?

Becky He's still here, isn't he?

Troy *enters.*

Leon (*sees* **Troy**) Charlie is gonna go ape when he catches sight of you.

Troy Don't try and put me under manners as well, Leon.

Leon What?

Becky Leon's right, where the fuck were yer?

Troy Why, did you miss me, Becky?

Becky Troy, I'd insult you, but you're not bright enough to notice.

Leon (*roars*) Oh!

Troy   Yeah, laugh it up, batty bwoi.

Leon   Where you going?

Troy   For a slash. Is that alright with you?

Leon   Can't.

Troy   Boy, don't tell me I can't –

Leon   Toilets got flooded, what's up with you?

Troy   Again? Who's doing this, man? Some nasty little white boy who don't know how to flush, that's who. I'm going outside.

Troy *leaves.*

Becky   Tell your mate to stop looking down my shirt.

Leon   Don't you like him?

Becky   Am I supposed to?

Leon   Most girls do.

Becky   Well, I'm not most girls, am I?

Leon   Look, yeah, cos I was wondering . . .

Charlie (*off*)   Becky?

Becky   What?

Charlie *comes out.*

Charlie   Key to the cash box, where is it, love?

Becky   Why?

Charlie   I wanna sort Tommy out with a sub, before we get it on with Palmer.

Becky   Dad, that's petty cash.

Charlie   Not now.

Becky   Yes now. You're not supposed to dip your hand in unless there's a good reason.

Charlie   This is a good reason. Key!

Becky   Bottom drawer.

Charlie   No it's not, I looked.

Becky   Hold up.

Becky *follows* **Charlie** *into the office.*

Troy *comes back.*

Leon   I'd have it on my toes if I were you, Troy.

Troy   ''ave it on my toes'?

Leon   Alright, but he ain't in the best of moods right now, trust me.

Troy   I thought he would have calmed down by now.

Leon   You missed a fight, Troy.

Troy   Yes, thank you, Leon, I know what I did.

Leon   The only reason you're here is cos of me, don't screw it up.

Troy   *Well, begging yer pardon, masa!* I can explain.

Leon   What you do this time?

Troy   Nuttin they weren't asking for.

Leon   Yer mug.

Troy   Why you talking like that? I got stopped. On the way to the fight.

Leon   So?

Troy   What you mean, so?

Leon   I mean, so? Ain't like it's the first.

Troy   So, that mek it alright then?

Leon   No.

Troy   They ca feel anyone's collar, so long as they are black?

Leon   They do, so why cry about it?

Troy   My mum was driving me, but they still had to pull us over, had to pad me down, right in front of her, mek me feel shame. If she hadn't stepped in, I woulda bust that coppers claart well and truly. Then she starts in wid there shit, saying I am like my dad, ca I lose my temper too much.

Leon   So you bin having a ruck with yer mum cos some dopey white copper was having it wid yer?

Troy   Why am I telling you, cos white must be right now, innit?

He grabs the bag. **Leon** *hits it.*

Troy   You know what, fuck it, I'm going to America.

Leon   What?

Troy   Mum wants me to go. She wants me to stay with my dad cos, according to her, I am out of control. I'm gonna say, fine, buy my ticket and I'm gone.

Leon   You don't mean that?

Troy   Why, you gonna miss me?

Leon   Move!

Troy   I always knew you were queer.

Leon   You're really gonna let them push you out?

Troy   I didn't say that. No one is pushing me to do anything, Leon. So relax. I go when I say. Mum, Babylon, they ain't chasing me out.

Becky *comes out of the office. She grabs her things like she is in a hurry.*

Becky   Sod this, I'm going to Mum's.

Leon   Becky?

Becky   What?

Leon   Have you seen *Conan the Barbarian*?

Becky   No.

Leon   It's showing at the Odeon.

Becky   Yeah?

Leon   I got a mate who works there, he sneaks me in so I don't have to pay, any time I like . . .

Becky   Leon, I'm walking out of the door. If you're going to ask me out, hurry up.

Leon   Will you go out with me?

Becky   If you're lucky.

Becky *leaves.*

Leon *has an enormous smug smile on his face.*

Troy   What was that about me not messing with the boss man's daughter? Yer fucking *ejut*!

Leon *gives him the finger.*

Lights on **Leon** *with a skipping rope.*

Leon   Next couple of fights can't come soon enough. I'm on a roll. I'm unstoppable. Now I have Eddie Barnham from Charlton in my sights. Eddie fights for the Fitzroy Lodge Club and is the current ABA champ! I do my fancy footwork as I step into the ring. I've got a small bunch of people following my fights now. I've got fans, Jesus! They're only calling my footwork 'The Leon Shuffle'! Oh man, Becky is in the crowd, I do the moonwalk as I give her a wave. Bin practising for months! Now the shuffle. Sugar Ray spin. I can see I've got him psyched, before I can lay a finger. I'm working him, still working him, still working . . . yes, I got him! Down he goes. Eddie's eating canvas. His arse ain't getting back up. (*Laughs.*) Oh, what is this? They're chanting my name now. Unreal. And the ref calls it!

A knockout in round one, my first ever! They give me the biggest cheer, as I'm crowned the new ABA Welterweight Champion, with the Leon Shuffle.

Leon *is in the gym with* **Becky** *and* **Troy**. *Scene begins with them in mid-conversation and* **Leon** *teaching* **Becky** *how to do his shuffle. James Brown music blaring from* **Leon**'s *ghetto blaster.*

Troy   Tune!

Leon   It is the truth, honest to Gods!

Becky   No way.

Leon   It was all planned.

Becky   You were lucky.

Leon   He was the one who was lucky, coming out of that ring alive. I took pity on that fool by knocking him out. No, no, you're doing it all wrong again.

Becky   Well, come on, genius, show me how.

Leon   Watch me. Stand straight. Legs apart. Lift up your right leg. Then point the toes of your right towards the floor. Then move your other leg, and slide like so. (*Does a moonwalk.*)

Becky   Nice.

Leon   You try it.

Troy   Why you bothering, she can't do it.

Leon   She can.

Troy   She's white.

Leon   Ignore him.

Becky   Ignore who?

Leon   Good one. Now, stand straight.

Becky   Legs apart.

Leon (*holds her leg*)   Lift up your right leg.

Becky (*enjoying this*)   Yeah?

Leon (*holds her right foot*)   Point these towards the floor.

Becky   Got it.

Leon   Then just *slide* with it.

Charlie *pops his head out.*

Charlie   Oi! What is that?

Leon (*panicking*)   Nothing, Chas! Bitta music, Chas, keeps me on my feet.

Charlie (*to* **Becky**)   What you doing here?

Becky   Moonwalking.

Charlie   Turn it off.

Leon   It's Michael Jackson, Chas.

Charlie   I don't care who it is – off.

Leon   But you can't turn him off.

Charlie   You just watch me.

Leon   But it's wicked. It keeps me sharp, I can feel the vibe.

Charlie   What is he saying to me?

Leon   Come on, Chas, put a bit of colour to yer life.

Charlie   Bitta wha?

Leon   I need him.

Charlie   Five minutes. This is a gym, not a club.

Troy   Yassir!

Charlie   Well, look who it ain't. You've decided to honour us with your presence at last. Where have you been?

Troy   Around.

Charlie   First you miss a fight, then I don't see you for months, but you think you can waltz back in here, like it never –

Troy   Well, tell the Babylon to leave me alone then.

Charlie   I'm not interested in any of that.

Troy (*aside*)   Just like a white man.

Charlie   Do I take it that you've come back here to apologise, that you want to fight again? What was that? I can't hear you.

Leon   Say yes.

Troy   Yes!

Charlie   What else?

Troy   Sorry!

Charlie   Well, thanks to the boy wonder here, I am in a forgiving mood. You be where I tell you to be, no excuses.

Troy   Yes, Charlie.

Charlie   Well, don't just stand there like a melt, get busy with it.

Troy   Working the bag now.

Charlie   That bag is working you, boy.

Troy (*aside*)   I ain't yer boy.

Leon   Oh man, leave it.

Charlie (*to* **Becky**)   You. Home!

Charlie *goes back into his office.*

Leon   How close was that?

Becky   You're not scared now are you, Leon? Big man like you.

Leon *yelps as* **Becky** *grabs his crotch.*

Leon   You wanna learn how to do this or what?

Becky *giggles.*

Leon   What now?

Becky   You're tickling me. (**Leon** *tickles her.*) Leon!

Tommy *enters. He sees* **Leon** *all over* **Becky***.*

Leon   Don't forget, just let your foot gently slide along the floor.

Becky   Like this?

Leon   Yeah, that's it, girl, that's it. Troy, watch!

Troy   Move.

Becky   Nothing to it!

Leon   Oh yeah!

Tommy *slams the door to his locker.*

Troy   You got summin to say, *Thomas*!

Tommy   Like yer meat burnt now, do yer?

Becky   What if I do?

Tommy   You make me sick.

Leon   Tommy, as much as we enjoy shooting the breeze wid yer –

Tommy   Listen to yourself, like yer one of the boys.

Leon   I don't think it would be wise to take this conversation much further. Need I say more?

Troy   Tell him, Leon.

Tommy (*to* **Becky**)   Chas is gonna have a stroke.

Becky   Dad doesn't need to know, it's only a bit of fun.

Tommy   You're gonna get a rep, girl.

Becky   Why are you packing your stuff? Are you leaving?

Tommy   Where is he, in his office?

Becky   You just let him down gently, alright?

Tommy *goes to* **Charlie**'s *office*.

Becky   Here we go again.

Leon   With what?

Sound of shouting from **Charlie**'s *office*.

Charlie   Moving onto who?

Tommy   No one, Chas, I just fancy a change.

Charlie   Was it Bishop?

Tommy   No, I said.

Charlie   I thought I told you to stay away. I'll handle him.

Tommy   What's there to handle? He's a top-notch promoter. He knows talent when he sees it.

Tommy, *quickly followed by* **Charlie**, *comes bursting out of the office*.

Charlie   He's turning yer head.

Tommy   What's so wrong with that? I'm fed up with you feeding me cast-offs.

Charlie   That's him talking, and you believe him? He'll toss you over his shoulder like a bleeding Coke can. Two years, you'll be nothing but a memory. Tommy?

Becky   Dad!

Charlie   Leave me, will yer?

Becky   Just let him go. You're making a scene.

Charlie   Come on, please?

Tommy   Palmer is a joke. I keep telling you. Bishop was laughing his arse off when I said you were dealing with him. Well, I ain't having anyone laughing at me.

Charlie You can't go. I'm your manager.

Tommy Not in writing, you're not.

Charlie Tell yer old man what yer doing.

Tommy Oh, here it comes.

Charlie See if he doesn't wallop yer, cos in our day –

Tommy Yes, that's it, Chas, good one, bore the arse out of me again with tales about you and him were Teddy boy kings, and all of this was your manor. The world's changing, you sad old tosspot, catch up, will yer? You just can't see what's under your nose. Too busy running after these lot.

Charlie I'll get rid of them then.

Tommy Do what you want, mate. I'm signing with Bishop.

Charlie Who's yer trainer?

Tommy Come on, Chas, don't do this.

Charlie Who?

Tommy He'll find me one.

Charlie What am I, a mirage? I can come with you then, as your trainer? Tommy?

Tommy Nobody rates you, Chas. I'm sorry, yeah?

Tommy *leaves.* **Charlie** *follows.*

Becky Where you going?

Charlie Out of my way, girl.

Becky If you go after him, I'm going back to Mum's, I swear. Don't beg.

Charlie I'm not begging, who do you think I am?

Charlie I was schoolboy's champion when he was nothing but a glint in the milkman's eye.

Becky That's right.

Charlie   I'm not a joke.

Becky   No one's saying that.

Charlie (*calls*)   You don't know what you're talking about, Tommy, people rate me.

Charlie *turns his head over to* **Troy** *and* **Leon**, *who are suddenly trying to look busy.*

Charlie (*to* Troy *and* Leon)   Having a good look?

Troy   No, Chas.

Leon   Just working out, Chas.

Charlie   You putting on weight, Leon?

Becky   Leave him, Dad.

Charlie   Look at him.

Leon   I ain't putting on weight, Chas.

Charlie   They could screen an episode of *Crossroads* on that arse.

Leon   Alright, I'll get it off.

Charlie   You've got the Olympics next year. Gonna get eaten alive.

Leon   I said I'll get it off, Chas. I'm not the one who's leaving you.

Charlie (*to* Troy)   As for you, throw a bloody punch in this gym as well as you do when you're out, or get out, you understand?

Becky   Dad, will you please calm down?

Charlie   Too bleeding soft, my trouble. Well, no more! Let's see some work for a change. Come on!

Becky   It's Tommy you're angry at, Dad.

Charlie   Nothing but a liberty, Becks.

Becky   A diabolical liberty.

Charlie   Jesus, I want a drink!

Becky   Don't you dare. You promised me, remember? Let it go, Dad.

Charlie   Fuck him, eh?

Becky   Fuck him. Come on.

Becky *takes him back into his office.*

Troy   'Throw a bloody punch'? I'll throw him a bloody punch. Like I did with that policeman.

Leon   Always love to chat, innit, Troy?

Troy   Excuse?

Leon   You can see how upset Charlie is and all you think about is yourself.

Troy   *Oh, well, please don't whip me, boss.*

Leon   Will you stop that?

Troy (*mimics*)   *I'm not the one leaving you, Chas.* If I didn't hear it wid my own ears, I would have never believed.

Leon   Just forget it.

Troy   I'm trying to. Trust me.

Leon   Tell me the truth.

Troy   What?

Leon   Do I look fat to you?

Troy *shoves the punchbag hard in* **Leon**'s *direction.*

Lights on **Leon**.

Leon   Something is going wrong, I've seen this Cuban kid fight, he ain't all that, he's as brittle as anything, truth be told. But summin's up here and it's all me. Every time I get inside, he's on me, like skin. Gotta get through somehow, but it's like he can read my mind. Should be giving him a dose of the Leon Shuffle by now, but I can't find my groove, shit!

Charlie (*from the ropes*)   Guard, Leon, your guard!

Leon *throws a punch.*

Charlie   Gimme more.

Leon   No way am I going home without a medal. I know I'm making dents here but this Cuban keeps on coming.

Charlie   Come on, boy, what you got?

Leon   This!

He lands a blow.

Oh! His left is down, he's stepping to the right, this is my chance, so I take it. I'm ready for more, stack 'em up, Chas. One by one, let's get them in here! Jamie Collins from Australia is my next victim. A piece of piss, I take him in out in two. Andrew Brookes? Having a laugh, mate. Ref stops it in one.

Charlie   Oh my boy! You brilliant gorgeous little boy!

Leon   I want more, need more.

Charlie   Let's be having yer!

Bell rings.

Leon   Quarter finals, Maxwell Glover, now we are talking. Reigning Olympic champion is Max. Now he's got a rep that's as big as a continent. Everyone reckons he's gonna retain the gold, And I've got a hard on this big, to take it from him.

Charlie   We're almost there Leon, I can smell it. You're gonna be the pride of Britain. Use your head. Focus!

Leon *does his shuffle. He then takes a blow.*

Leon   Didn't see that one coming.

Charlie What was that, I said focus!

Leon Who is this geezer, The Flash?

Leon *takes another blow.*

Leon What again?

Leon *takes yet another blow.*

Leon Oh, this is getting a bit silly now.

Charlie Come on, Leon, please, don't do this to me.
I want that medal.

Leon I gotta do something.

Leon *lands a punch.*

Leon And he's down. Whose Flash now? Who are you
now? Here it comes, ca hear it now, crowds are chanting my
name, millions watching me on the telly, love it! Hear that
yer Flash wanke—

Charlie Corner! Now!

Leon I don't know why the ref's counting? He's down, he's
out. (*Hears the chants.*) Here they go. (*Calls.*) Love you too!

Charlie What, no shuffle?

Leon (*panting*) I can't do it. My body, it's all –

Charlie Fucked? You know why? Cos he didn't just stand
there, whilst you were prancing around like some poof.

Leon What you yelling for, I'm through to the semis,
aren't I?

Charlie By this much! You were dropping your guard.
Try getting that into your head the next time you do a
Michael Jackson!

Leon Oh, I've had this! You're spoiling it.

Leon *leaves.*

Charlie   I'm not spoiling it. I'm keeping you on the ground. Oi, don't you walk away from me. When are you going to start thinking? I mean, it's only the bleeding Olympics so no pressure then. Leon? Are you receiving me?

It is night-time. Sounds of a police car wailing its siren from outside. **Charlie** *is alone onstage, cleaning the ring with great care. It is almost as if the ring is all that he has left in the world. He jumps when he hears a sound.*

Charlie   Hello? I said hello? Look, this isn't funny, alright. Now who's there? (*Hears more noise.*) Alright, you wanna get tricky with me . . .

Charlie *goes into his office.*

Leon *comes running in, out of breath. He clasps his hands, he is in pain.*

Charlie *comes bursting out of his office waving a baseball bat.*

Charlie   Well, come on, let's have yer!

Leon   Chas, don't.

Charlie   This is my gym!

Leon   It's me.

Charlie   What the bleeding hell are you playing at?

Leon   Chas, just put the bat down, yeah, please.

Charlie   It's the middle of the night, boy.

Leon   I didn't think you'd be here.

Charlie   Evidently.

Leon   Why ain't you at home?

Charlie   None of your business. Is there trouble on the Estate again?

Leon   I was just going home. Got caught up in it.

Charlie   So you thought you'd hide in here?

Leon I'm not hiding.

Charlie So what are you doing?

Leon Like I'm scared or summin.

Charlie *Jesus H.* You're a touchy little git, aren't yer? It's not about being scared, it's about being smart. You did the right thing, coming here. I mean, listen. Have you seen the news? It's kicking off in Tottenham now. You lot.

Leon What you mean, 'you lot'?

Charlie Oh, calm down, I didn't mean . . .

Leon I am. Jus don't say –

Charlie Do they really think they have the essentials to take on Maggie? What planet are they on? She kicked the argys into touch without losing a wink of sleep. She walked all over the miners like they weren't even there, and they ain't that little bit impressed?

Leon Stroll on, Chas.

Charlie Burning cars, smashing up shops. If the old bill can't put a stop to this, she'll call in the army, then it's game over, boy.

Leon They're just vex.

Charlie 'Vex'?

Leon Yeah, Chas, *vex*! You don't know what it's like.

Charlie I don't want to know. And neither should you.

Leon We get Babylon in our face all the time.

Charlie 'Babylon'?

Leon Police, come on, Chas.

Charlie Speak English then.

Leon It's like they wanna beat up on every black kid in London now, make out we don't belong.

Charlie   Don't give me that pony. You were born here, of course you belong.

Leon   Tell that to *Maggie's boys* then. What did they think was gonna happen?

Charlie   What's wrong with your hand?

Leon   Nothing.

Charlie   Show me it.

Leon   Why?

Charlie   Cos I said so.

Leon   I'm alright, Chas.

Charlie   So why you shaking? Let's have a butcher's if it's nothing. Show me your hands.

Leon   Just don't get mad.

Charlie *checks his hands.*

Charlie   Bruising.

Charlie *squeezes* **Leon**'s *hand. He yelps.*

Leon   I can explain, yeah.

Charlie   After all I've just said. What are you trying to do to me?

Leon   Weren't my fault. I didn't mean for it to happen.

Charlie   You didn't mean what to happen? Leon? Don't make me brain you. What did you do?

Leon   We got chased by coppers, me and Troy.

Charlie   Troy!

Leon   They tried to nick us, we didn't do anything. Troy went mad at them.

Charlie   What are you trying to do to me?

Leon   Nothing.

Charlie   Tommy warned me, he did. And others. I let him go and all I've got left is you lot, doing all sorts!

Leon   It's not me.

Charlie   It's all you're good for. Like you can't help yourselves. Like it's in your blood. Clear out your locker.

Leon   Chas?

Charlie   Clear it out now. Every boy I have lets me down. Why should you be any different?

Leon   I got you a medal, didn't I?

Charlie   And if you had listened to me, it would have been Gold.

Leon   You are never happy.

Charlie (*points to his office*)   I am in there, working my bollocks off to keep this place alive. I might as well save myself the agg. I give you boys my all, get you ready to turn pro and all you do is let me down, bloody sick of it.

Leon   Turn pro? Are you turning me pro?

Charlie   You've had interest.

Leon   About time!

Charlie   Tommy's people want to set up a fight.

Leon   Well, come then, let's have it.

Charlie   I thought you were ready.

Leon   I am ready.

Charlie   You broke the rules, boy.

Leon   But I can beat him though.

Charlie   You fight in the ring, nowhere else. Fighting coppers! How can I train you now . . . ?

Leon   As soon as it kicked off, I got out of there, Chas, I swear. All I did was try and stop Troy going mad.

Charlie   Why fight in the first place?

Leon   He made me. I didn't know what to say.

Charlie   'No' would have done it.

Leon   You don't say no to Troy.

Charlie   Since when are you scared of him?

Leon   I ain't!

Charlie   You gotta drop him.

Troy *enters*.

Leon   Come on, Chas. He's my bro.

Charlie   Who is holding you back. Don't be a nobody.

Troy   So, what happened, Leon?

Charlie   Well, speak of.

Troy   'Bout you running out on me like that.

Leon   I didn't run out on you.

Troy   You left me with them.

Leon   No I didn't.

Troy   So where were you?

Leon   I got lost; I was looking for yer.

Troy   Yer fucking lickle pussy!

Charlie   That's enough.

Troy   He bloody ran, man, turned his back on me.

Charlie   Not my problem.

Troy   Well, nose out then.

Charlie   Oi!

*Troy shoves **Charlie** when he grabs his arm.*

Troy   Don't ever touch me, yeah?

Leon   Troy?

Troy   I don't want no white man touching me from now on.

Charlie   Going off on one like you always do.

Troy   Get out of my face, Chas.

Charlie   You wanna take me on, boy?

Troy   That's the last time you're ever calling me 'boy'.

Charlie   Good, cos I want you out. You're no fighter. Not in here.

Troy   Fine then, mi gone! Leon, you coming?

Charlie   Tell him.

Leon   Charlie, don't.

Troy   Tell me what?

Charlie (*to* **Leon**)   Somebody or nobody, make your choice.

Charlie *goes back to his office.*

Troy   Waiting.

Leon   I'm not going with you, Troy. Wanna hang here.

Troy *empties his locker.*

Troy   Look at yer, so happy to be his bitch.

Leon   Turn that in.

Troy   Turn that in? *Arthur Daley, little dodgy maybe, but underneath, he's alright!* You stay wid the white women, like yer dad. Let that hoo Becky run you around like a dog.

Leon   Oi!

Troy   Once she's had enough of tasting the black man, yer done.

Leon   You wanna slap? I'll deck yer.

Troy   Ca yer the fighter. Mr Big Man now!

Leon   I ain't pissing about.

Troy (*mocks*)   *This time next year, we'll be millionaires!*

Leon   I know who I am!

Troy (*screams*)   Nigga, what happened to you?!

Troy *grabs his bag and heads for the door.*

Leon   I know who I am, Troy!

Bell rings.

Lights on **Leon**.

Leon   Oh yes, this is bandit country, without a shadow.
All these crowds, all white, pale faces, It's spot the darkie.
They're cheering Tommy on, telling him to bury me.
That's what they want, ever since the Brixton riots,
Broadwater Farm, they wanna see a *fucking wog* buried,
put in his place. I'm the main course and they are serving
me up!

Tommy (*off*)   No way am I losing to a black man!

Leon   Yes, bring it on, you fucking cockney wide boy
redneck! Let them all watch, I'm gonna smash you back
to Bow.

Bell rings.

Tommy   Well, come on, golly.

Leon   Look at this fool, thinks he can spook me?

Tommy   Come and get me, monkey!

Tommy *lands a punch.*

Leon This motherfucker has some pain coming.

Leon *comes out fighting.*

Tommy Wiggle yer tail. Come on!

Leon Don't rise. See his game. Be smart now.

Tommy Can't you take it, black boy?

Leon (*snaps*) Jab to his face. And another.

Tommy *lands a couple of shots.*

Leon Fucking crowd, hear them with their do *the spade*! *Do the spade*! (*He lands a blow.*) Yes, how you like that jab to the body, Thomas? That's what I'm talking about. (*He does the shuffle.*) Yeah! (*He feels something at the back of his head.*) What the fuck? What, they throwing bottles at me now? Gotta finish this.

Tommy Jig a boo.

Leon Second he says that, I can see him, leaving himself wide open. Thank you very much, *Thomas*! (*Continues to punch.*) I ain't stopping for nothing! Hear them now, cussing me like you wouldn't believe. Come on, come on! So, what was that then, Tommy, you ain't losing to a black man? This black man here, this same black man who's giving you a proper spanking, you, right now? Oh my dear!

Tommy *falls. It is a knockout. The bell rings.* **Leon** *has won. Crowd jeers.*

Leon How you like that? Oh yeah. (*Yells at crowd.*) What, you ripping out seats now? I ain't moving. I ain't moving. That all you got? Come on, come on, give it to me.

He sees **Tommy** *going to his corner, saying something in* **Charlie's** *ear.*

Leon (*sees* **Charlie** *leaving*) Chas, where you going, Chas? (*To* **Tommy**.) What you say to him?

Tommy   Apart from you having his little girl, not a thing.

Leon   Chas? Chas? Where are you going? Hold up! Oh, fucking press! Can't they see that I want to talk to Chas? (*Takes a question.*) No, what you talking about? He didn't run out on me, he didn't run out on me, he musta thought I was right behind him, he'll be here, I just won the fight of my life, my first professional fight . . . I don't know where he is. No, I don't hate those people, I feel sorry for them. Charlie will be here, he's coming. Charlie ain't like that, he don't think like them. He doesn't! No, no, no, Charlie Maggs is still my trainer, and I'm his boy.

Act Two

Gym.

Leon *is with* **Becky** *and* **Squid** *in the gym.* **Squid** *is opening and reading some hate mail.*

Squid (*reads letter*) 'What kind of a black man would run after a white man after he leave him behind like that? Answer, no kind!'

Becky Don't read him any more.

Squid Oh, yer gonna love this one.

Becky Mr Davidson?

Squid 'How could you stand there like that, smiling, letting them call you monkey? You should have walked out of the ring in protest.'

Becky Leon, don't listen.

Squid No, Leon, listen. (*Reads another.*) 'You call yourself black? Even your manager had to walk away in shame.' (*Reads another.*) 'You been kissing the white man's arse for so long, you are starting to like it?' (*Reads another.*) 'The Leon Shuffle? Why don't you shuffle on back to the dole queue?' That's my favourite.

Becky They are jealous, ignore them.

Squid What business have you being wid a white woman?

Becky Have you finished?

Squid That's black people for you. Nuttin but crabs in a pot. When one gets to the top, all the others want to do is drag it back down.

Leon Ain't no one pulling me down.

Squid So it now you decide to turn man?

Becky   Why can't you leave him alone?

Squid   Is who you chat to, gal?

Becky   He's upset, can't you see?

Leon   I'm not upset.

Becky   Your son, remember?

Leon   Becks, I'm alright.

Squid   You grind her yet?

Leon   What?

Squid   She, you grind her yet?

Becky   Unbelievable.

Leon   Dad, don't talk about her like that, please?

Becky   Please?

Squid   That mean no. My God!

Leon   Don't.

Squid   A dog do better dan you.

Leon   Dad?

Becky   Don't talk to him.

Leon   What you mean, don't talk to him?

Squid   You best step it up, bwoi, this is one gal who want fuck.

Leon   I have actually.

Becky   Leon!

Leon   Nuff times. What, you don't believe me?

Squid   Alright, alright, you the man.

Becky   I am still right here, you know, if you don't mind. And if my dad heard what you were saying now –

Squid   Him what? Go run and hide like he's doing right now is what. You nuh see his rass for days, child.

Leon   Dad, she's worried, rein it in, will yer!

Squid   It's me one here, not him. 'bout him run out, leave my son behind. You tink I want put down my own boy? I'm just keeping him real. A whole heap of other boys like him coming through, I don't want him standing like fool compared to dem.

Leon   What other boys?

Squid   Yer old friend, Troy, for one.

Leon   Troy?

Squid   You nuh hear? Him just gone from amateur to pro, in the shortest time ever in the States.

Leon   Troy? Boxing?

Squid   Him work out in the Kronk.

Leon   The Kronk? *The Kronk?*

Squid   Sparring with Hearns there.

Leon   Hit man Hearns? No way.

Squid   So I hear.

Leon   Bullshit, Dad, that is bullshit.

Squid   Don't shoot me, him mudda tell me. She also say one day he'll come back.

Leon   Let him.

Squid   Him say he go win everything. Be the first black British man to win the belt.

Leon   He gave up being a Brit when he went to the States.

Squid   You be a fool to bet against him. He is what I'd call a sure thing.

Leon   Alright, what is it?

Squid   Nuttin, son.

Leon   What have I done wrong now?

Squid   I said nuttin. Except, say, go mess up my vibe. Go beat Tommy, the British number-one challenger, I mean, what the hell was that?

Becky   You bet on Tommy?

Leon   You didn't bet on me?

Squid   The boy has never lost a fight, you mad? Of course mi bet on him. And you had to go tump his arse fer him, innit?

Leon   What round?

Squid   What the hell difference it mek? It was only a bet. Nuttin personal.

Leon   What round did you bet on, Dad?

Squid   Oh cha rass, boy!

Leon   What round were you expecting to see me lying on the ground, wid my head busted?

Squid   The third. And it weren't like that. You go cry now?

Becky   I think you had better go, Mr Davidson.

Squid   Gal polite, you see. 'm not going anywhere, child.

Charlie *comes in, drunk.*

Charlie   What have I missed?

Leon   Here he is!

Becky   Dad, where have you been?

Charlie   Business.

Squid   Yeah, man, I can smell the business!

Becky   Oh, Dad, no. You promised.

Charlie Come on, Squid, you know the rules. No family members. Alright! So, get out.

Squid Excuse me?

Charlie If you wouldn't mind.

Squid Him my boy.

Charlie And this is my gym. No losers allowed.

Squid Hey, is who the hell you tink –

Leon Dad, just walk away. He didn't mean it . . .

Squid I ask him a question, why you so soff, boy?

Leon (*offers him some notes*) Here!

Squid What dis?

Leon Just take it and go.

Squid You want discuss our business in front of dem?

Leon Not now, alright.

Squid So, he get in my face and all you do is –

Leon Dad, will you please just go?

Squid (*feeling hurt, he snatches the money*) You want to grover to them, be my guest, I'm gone!

Squid *storms out.*

Charlie Oh dear!

Becky I've been frantic for days, I even called the police, and you've been out on the bloody piss!

Leon You alright, Chas?

Charlie You know, thirty years, Leon. Thirty years, I would have strung you up if you so much as even looked at her. Now you lot think you can do what you want.

Leon Stroll on, Chas.

Charlie Don't call me Chas. Don't say *stroll on* like yer one of the chaps.

Leon Why are you getting all narked for?

Charlie I said stop it. Last to know about this, was I?

Becky What difference would that make?

Charlie A backhander is what you need, girl.

Becky You haven't got the guts.

Leon Come on, Chas, you wouldn't.

Charlie No, I wouldn't do that.

Leon Course.

Charlie Wouldn't call the Old Bill when you and Troy broke into my office. Wouldn't have told his mum to piss right off when she came here begging to let you off. Wouldn't smash Tommy and his dad in the face for laughing at me, right in my face. You couldn't keep yer legs closed, you had to open them up wide for the likes of him.

Leon Hey, Chas, come on?

Charlie (*shoves him off*) Last fight I had in the ring, Leon, was in 1972, but in your case, I will come out of retirement so bleeding fast, I'll leave you behind. Don't you ever touch me.

Leon Alright, I'm not touching yer.

Charlie Just piss off, alright? Get out of my gym. What are you standing there for? You heard what I said. Get out.

Leon You don't mean that.

Charlie I mean it this time. I don't wanna see your face again.

Leon Oh, go with Bishop like Tommy then, shall I? Watch you and the gym go under without me? I've seen you with all them final demands.

Charlie   This is still my gym!

Leon   You need me.

Becky   Leon?

Leon   Come on, Chas, this ain't you, it's the JD talking.

Charlie   I said out.

Leon   You don't want me to go, and I ain't going. Yer like a dad to me.

Charlie (*in a rage*)   BUT I'M NOT YER FUCKING DAD, AM I? I'M NOT YER DAD, LEON, I NEVER FUCKING WAS, I DIDN'T ASK TO BE. How can I be yer dad? Have you ever heard the like? Well, have yer? You think cos you've got crowds cheering you on now, I call you son, that makes you one of us? Believe it, Leon, believe it cos its true. We hate you.

Leon   I don't believe yer.

Charlie   So why am I saying it?

Leon   Cos you wanna believe it.

Charlie   Who cares?

Leon   I do! You'll never get anyone as good as me again. You know that. I'll never have anyone as good as you. You want proof? Alright, be my manager as well as my trainer. We'll make it official, put it in writing.

Charlie   Bunch of coffee-coloured kids running around, calling me grandad. I'm not having that.

Becky   Shut up, Dad.

Charlie   You're living in a dream world.

Leon   Chas, did you hear me?

Becky   Leon?

Leon   I'm gonna get you your first world title, yer gonna throw it all away because of me and her?

Charlie   I want it as bad as you.

Leon   Well, come on then!

Becky   Leon, he can't.

Leon   Just wait. Chas?

Charlie   Alright then, alright. I'll be your trainer-manager.

Leon   Sorted!

Charlie   Just leave my girl alone.

Leon   What?

Charlie   You wanna screw around with slags like yer old man, that's your business but not with her. Give her up, right now, alright?

Becky   Dad, you bastard.

Charlie   That's the deal. Take it or leave. Well?

Becky   Come on, Leon let's go. Leon?

Leon   You wanna wait outside for a bit, Becks?

Becky   What?

Leon   You wanna wait outside for a bit?

Becky   No, I don't.

Leon   Just for a bit.

Becky   Are you coming with me, yes or no?

Leon   Just wait outside for a bit, Becks, please?

Becky   Stop saying that.

Leon   Just for a bit.

Becky   Don't do it.

Leon   Just for a bit. How many more times –

Becky *slaps his face.*

Leon Just for a bit.

Becky *slaps him again repeatedly.*

Leon Becks? It's like what you said once, a little bit of fun.

Becky I know what I said.

Leon So, what then?

Becky You know what, read those letters Leon. Read every one. Believe every word, cos it's true.

Becky *leaves.*

Charlie Fiery, like her mum. That's the Irish in her.

Leon Are you for real?

Charlie You just gonna stand there or work out?

Leon She's gone, Chas.

Charlie She's my blood. She'll be back.

Charlie *throws him a pair of gloves.*

Charlie Get to work.

Lights on **Leon**.

Leon Charlie set up a fight for me against Paul Kieron from Leeds. Royal Albert Hall, thousands of seats, it was a seventy thirty split seeing as Kieron was a former world-title holder. I take Kieron out in five. Three months later, I'm there again, battering the hell out of Noah Hunter in the fourth. And all we got was a forty split. The nerve! Earls Court next, take on the UK champ, Shaun Callum, it was a fifty fifty split, but it took me nine rounds to get that belt off him, and then six in the rematch, which is where the real money is and I ain't lying, we cleaned up! Spring of '87, Wembley Arena, fighting Paul Edwards, and, yes, finally, this time we are the ones calling the shots, setting the pace, walking away with the biggest purse. Seventy thirty in our favour and, I swear, I can almost smell that dinero. I get the drop on Edwards in the third, all too easy. Oh yes, without a doubt, I'm in my prime now. Money is rolling in. My face on is on the front page of the *Boxing News*. Giving Chas his first European title belt after I gave that Kraut Werner a proper spanking. Oh yes! Now I have papers, magazines, telly interviewing me nearly every week now. Asking me if I'm ever going for the world title? Let me get this straight. Two title belts. Ten wins. Six knockouts does the Pope live in Rome? Of course I am going for the world title! I can't be touched, I won't be touched.

Leon *is back in the gym with* **Becky**.

Becky   You have to stop this, Leon.

Leon   Told you already, girl, I don't know what you're talking about.

Becky   I know it's you.

Leon   Becks, believe me.

Becky   Calling me all the time, hanging up when you hear my voice, was annoying.

Leon   Not me.

Becky   Insulting my boyfriend when he answers the phone, was just plain childish.

Leon   Not me!

Becky   Now you're stalking me?

Leon   No.

Becky   This stops now. Are you listening?

Leon   What makes you think it's me?

Becky   One of my neighbours saw you lurking around earlier. 'Black kid, he looked just like Leon Davidson,' she says.

Leon   Nice!

Becky   She wanted to call the police. Now she wants an autograph. (**Leon** *chuckles*.) Why are you doing this?

Leon   If it was me, did you ever think that maybe it was because I'm looking out for you? It's a rough area you are living in, Becks.

Becky   I've got Simon looking after me.

Leon   He sounds like a bender.

Becky   Leon, what is going on in that head?

Leon   Like I got time to be chasing after you.

Becky   This stops, right now.

Leon   Too busy larging it in the West End to chase after you.

Becky   Do you understand me?

Leon   I'm one of the faces, girl.

Becky   No more.

Leon   Voice down. Unless you want Charlie coming out.

Becky   It's like I'm talking to a total stranger. I'm going.

Leon   Meeting *Simon*?

Becky   Yes, Leon, I am meeting *Simon*. We are having dinner.

Leon   How posh.

Becky   It's only a pizza.

Leon   It's the way you say it. Is he white, Simon?

Becky   Yes.

Leon   So, you finally give up the taste of a black man?

Becky   That's Troy talking.

Leon   It's getting dark. I can drive you home in my spanking new car if you like?

Becky   I thought it might be yours.

Leon   Did you think it was Charlie's?

Becky *smiles at the thought.*

Leon   There it is. You know, your smile just lights me up, whenever I see it. It always did, you know that? So, you like it then, the motor?

Becky   It's nice.

Leon   It's an Aston Martin. You know, like James Bond.

Becky   Yes, I know. Expensive.

Leon   I can afford it now.

Becky   As long you're being careful.

Leon   Of course. Charlie's investing my money. Looking after it.

Becky   Charlie? Bit risky, isn't it?

Leon   Why?

Becky   This is my dad we're talking about.

Leon   If I didn't know any better, I'd say, *Rebecca*, that you were caring about me.

Becky   It's your money.

Leon   Trying to ruin my fun.

Becky   Forget it.

Leon   I know what I'm doing.

Becky   Sorry!

Leon   Cos it was the best feeling in the world when I walked right into the dealer's shop. I slam the money down and I goes, 'That one, I want that one.' You like? You wanna?

Becky   I am really happy for you.

Leon   So let me take you for a spin in it.

Becky   I thought you were just going to drop me home?

Leon   We'll take a nice drive over the bridge.

Becky   Will you stop?

Leon   Stop? Stop what?

Becky   You broke my fucking heart.

Leon   Calm down, girl.

Becky   Strutting around like it was nothing. You're not even sorry for what you did, are you? I loved you.

Leon   You loved the thrill.

Becky   Then I loved you.

Leon   You don't want a ride, cool. That is fine. I got smart shoes, pukka suits. New telly with a video. What I need you for?

Becky   Exactly.

Leon   Page Three girl with a fine pair of Bristols is what I need.

Becky (*takes out a piece of paper from the bag*)   Could you sign this please?

Leon   What is it?

Becky   Autograph for my neighbour, remember?

Leon *signs it.*

Leon   Coulda least wait for yer dad. He'll be out in a sec.

Becky   How is he?

Leon   Same.

Becky   He's not drinking, is he?

Leon   Maybe, maybe not.

Becky Please, Leon.

Leon Ask him yourself if you're that bothered.

Becky Tell me.

Leon No. Not that I know of.

Becky Thank you.

Leon (*rattles his car keys*) Last chance. The car, goes like a dream, Becky, it's so good you'll cream yourself.

Becky That's disgusting.

Leon Only joking, calm down.

Becky Leon?

Leon Oh, what now?

Becky This isn't you.

Becky *tries to go as quickly as possible as* **Charlie** *enters, having shown* **Ray** *around the gym.* **Charlie** *shows him a picture of his younger self, fighting.*

Charlie There's me again. 1968. Taken when I fought Curtis Cokes. Fast fucker. I landed a perfect left hook on for him in the first round then he – (*Sees* **Becky**.) Becky? Becky, love?

Becky Leave me, Dad, don't say a word.

Charlie Oh, babe, come on.

Becky No.

Charlie Darling, please . . .

Becky *goes.*

Charlie When were you planning on telling me she was here?

Leon She don't wanna know, Chas.

Charlie That's not what I asked. You should have told me.

Leon   Well, I didn't, get over it.

Charlie   You what?

Leon   You deaf?

Charlie   Listen –

Ray   Are we happy here?

Charlie   Of course. So sorry. Where was I?

Ray   Do you think we could hurry this . . . ?

Charlie   . . . Oh yes, Cokes. Now he was fast, made me bleed. No other fighter has ever done that to me, before or since. It was an honour. Did you know, he was never knocked out in his professional career?

Ray   No, I didn't.

Charlie   He was class. A gent. Unlike a lot of lads who fight nowadays – too much mouth. It's all about the dinero now, the money. Thank you, *Maggie*.

Ray   Not for my Troy. It's the smell of the ring. The thrill of a fight, the feeling before the first-round bell, that drives him. Crazy nigga would fight for nothing if I tell him to.

Charlie   How did you find him?

Ray   Detroit. Working at some gas station. This white cop caught a couple of black kids stealing from the store, he was roughing them pretty bad.

Charlie   Here it comes.

Ray   Troy grabbed the cop, knocked his ass into the middle of next week. He got busted, so I bailed him.

Charlie   Boy never learns.

Ray   Oh he learns. Ever since that prick of a father ran out on him, he had no choice but to learn. The way he hit – *whoa!* I took his ass straight to the Kronk. Those hands were meant for something other than cleaning men's rooms.

Leon (*chuckles*)   If he had asked, I would have lent him my mop.

Ray   Say what?

Leon   Just tell him, he'll know what I mean.

Ray   Right, OK.

Leon   I bet I know what he says about me.

Ray   I bet you don't.

Leon   Don't believe a word now. What does he say?

Ray   As a matter of fact, he's never mentioned you.

Leon   You lie.

Ray   Not once, babe.

Leon   You didn't know I knew him?

Ray   Not until just now.

Leon   He's been in America, you been training him how long, he's never mentioned me?

Ray   Nope.

Leon   He's been slagging me off in the papers since he got here, calling me Uncle Tom.

Ray   That's nothing personal. Just business.

Leon   I'm fine about it. But he never said?

Ray   I'm sorry.

Leon   You know, fuck him.

Leon *goes at it on the speed bag.*

Ray   So, we ready to do this, Charles?

Charlie   Oh, we are more than ready, Mr Reid.

Ray   But I think you and your boy here need to go back to bed and wake up again.

Charlie   Why is that? It was a perfectly good offer.

Ray   Floyd and Stephens were the two best challengers to the title – Troy beat their asses.

Charlie   Yeah, but I think –

Ray   Well, I never think, I just do. Now, I'm hungry, so can we finish this please? Come on now.

Charlie   What are you suggesting?

Ray   For you to get real, Charles.

Charlie   I believe I am.

Ray   Good. You can start by bringing that number down.

Charlie   Hang on.

Ray   Capiche? Come on, I want eat.

Charlie   I saw the Stephens fight.

Ray   Uh – huh?

Charlie   Well, forgive me for saying so, and no offence here –

Ray (*getting impatient*)   Yeah, yeah, yeah.

Charlie   Troy was lucky, by this much, to get it on points.

Ray   And Floyd?

Charlie   Yeah, he wasn't bad.

Ray   *Wasn't bad?* What fight were you watching, Charles?

Charlie   It's Charlie, please?

Ray   How long you been a trainer?

Charlie   Eleven years.

Ray   My boy outflanked him with every move. Troy is the real deal. Now, here is the news. Why don't you go back to that nice little office of yours, try coming up with a figure you know you can live with? And I promise you, I will say yes to it.

Charlie   Well, that's good, I'd appreciate that . . .

Ray   Just as long as it isn't something that I don't want to say yes to.

Leon   I don't see Troy wearing two belts.

Ray   Pardon me?

Leon   I don't even see him wearing one belt. It's me that's wearing them.

Ray   That's it, that all you got?

Leon   You need us, Ray.

Charlie   Leon, let me deal with this.

Leon   And you know it, so keep up.

Ray   Young man, the only thing I need to keep up is my dick. What the hell is this, Charles?

Charlie   My apologies, Mr Reid.

Leon   Mister?

Charlie   Bit excited, that is all. Why don't you step back into my office? We can discuss this . . .

Ray   Rollins will come to us in time, we don't need you.

Leon   Fine, forget Troy, I'll have Rollins to myself.

Ray   You think you can win? Then you take him. Better for us. Rollins, you, don't matter, Troy will whup all yer asses.

Leon   You will have to negotiate with me.

Charlie   With us!

Leon   Knowing I'm world champion.

Ray   Not if you lose the rematch.

Leon   Never gonna happen.

Ray   Maybe, but Troy will take it from you, and that *will* happen.

Charlie   As I said, shall we . . . ?

Ray   Sixty/forty in our favour.

Leon   Sixty-five/thirty-five, to us.

Ray   Get the fuck out of here.

Charlie   Hang on, be fair, he is loved over here.

Ray   He and his *shuffle* don't mean jack in the US of A.

Leon   I'm the UK and European champion!

Ray   Fuck it, I'm done here.

Ray goes to leave.

Charlie   We'll take it, sixty/forty.

Leon   What?

Charlie   I said we'll take it.

Leon   Chas? Are you mad?

Ray   Well, that is music to my ears. Oh yes. Now, if you fine gentlemen will excuse me, cos I've got so many places to be. My people will talk to your people, and we will get this party started. It's going to be one hell of a night, thank you, Charles, Leon! Let's rumble!

Ray leaves.

Leon   What are you doing?

Charlie   What am I doing? Why did you do *that*?

Leon   You were fucking it up.

Charlie   Watch yer mouth, boy, you're in my house. Now, you have to tread carefully with the likes of Reid, he's top-notch.

Leon   You were taking it up the arse.

Charlie   And you were showing us up. Are you listening to me? There is more going on here than just you and Troy. If you don't win, this place goes under and that's a fact.

Leon   What do you mean, 'go under'? I thought we were raking it in.

Charlie   Don't you read the papers, boy?

Leon   Yeah, I read the bloody papers.

Charlie   Recession? Stock market?

Leon   Oh no, you didn't.

Charlie   It'll be alright.

Leon   Every penny?

Charlie   It will be alright, I said.

Leon   Fucking hell, Chas!

Charlie   Maggie will sort it.

Leon   Never mind bloody Maggie. The money!

Charlie   We'll get it back. Once you've beaten Troy, we'll have the title in our sights, we'll be set for life.

Leon   We? Why should I help you now?

Charlie   I've seen the way you spend money, Leon. That bloody car outside! You are in the shit as well. You don't honestly think 40% is enough to cover all of our debts, do yer?

Leon   So, why agree?

Charlie   It was better than nothing. He was half way out the door because of you. So leave me alone and let me do it.

Charlie   And don't you ever keep Becky away from me again.

Leon   Fuck Becky!

Charlie   She's my girl.

Leon   Unbelievable.

Charlie   You don't decide for me. Are we clear?

Leon Fuck you, telling me what to do any more. Just know, I took you with me, when no one else would. I got you onto the coaching team at the Olympics, even though everyone was telling me not to. You know why? Cos no one rates you! I'm all you've got. I'm gonna save you, gonna save this gym, and you're gonna be on your knees thanking me for it.

Leon and **Troy** *are on the phone talking to each other*.

Troy Yeah, who dis? Hello? You there, somebody?

Leon It's me, Troy.

Troy And who might you be?

Leon Leon.

Troy *Leon?*

Leon Don't piss about.

Troy Leon Davidson! I'm honoured. So, what can I do for you, Leon Davidson?

Leon I just fancied a chat.

Troy I don't think you and I have anything to talk about.

Leon Troy, it's me. You can drop the act.

Troy This isn't an act.

Leon Calling me an Uncle Tom, what's that about?

Troy (*grunts*) That was business. Talk to Ray.

Leon Troy? Just hold up will yer, Troy? What's the bleeding hurry.

Troy What do you want, fool?

Leon Just for us to think for a minute.

Troy About what?

Leon The way it was.

Troy   I don't have time for this.

Leon   Troy, what's so wrong with kicking back a little, like we used to? Hang out and that? Look at us, can you believe this shit? I got a penthouse overlooking the Arndale Centre. Eight years ago you and me was rampaging through that place, stealing records from Our Price. (*Chuckles.*) You remember that?

Troy   No.

Leon   How can you not remember that, Troy? The security guards were chasing us all down Wandsworth High Street! We had to drop all the records and tapes.

Troy   I just don't. So, are we done?

Leon   Old times, mate, best time of times, it was like it was the only time for when shit made sense. Did you ever think then we would be where we are now?

Troy   I don't think about the past.

Leon   Is that why you didn't tell Ray anything about me? Like I never existed? I want the title, Troy.

Troy   Don't beg.

Leon   I ain't begging!

Troy   You talking like a bitch.

Leon   I thought I was talking to my mate.

Troy   I'm not your mate. Now, are we done here?

Leon   Oh, come on, Troy, don't be like that –

Troy *hangs up on him.*

Leon   You're still my – (*Realises he has been cut off.*)

Leon *is alone by himself in the gym. That phone conversation with* **Troy** *has clearly got to him. He takes out a roll of hand-wrap from his locker and begins wrapping his hands.* **Squid** *enters.*

Squid   How you doing, boy?

Leon   Dad, you shouldn't be here.

Squid   Yeah, I know.

Leon   Charlie's rules.

Squid   Hey, claart to Charlie's rules, yeah? What kind of a world are we living when I can't even come say hello to my boy before him have the biggest fight of his life? Wish him luck?

Leon   Seriously?

Squid   Look, I know I can be a bit much sometimes.

Leon   Sometimes?

Squid   You, my boy, I want make my peace wid you.

Leon   You come here to tell me that?

Squid   You deaf? So, that alright wid you?

Leon   It's alright.

Squid   You want help?

Leon   You know how?

Squid *helps* **Leon** *with wrapping his hand*.

Leon   No, you gotta wrap it over the back of my wrist.

Squid   OK.

Leon   Then over the back of my hand with it.

Squid   How many times?

Leon   Four.

Squid   One, two, three, four.

Leon   Just before you do a fifth.

Squid   I do this, up through the finger, then under the thumb.

Leon   Smart-arse.

Squid   How's that?

Leon   Good. Thanks.

Squid   So, how you feel?

Leon   Ripe!

Squid   So, what's your prediction for the fight?

Leon (*Mr T. impression*)   Pain!

They chuckle.

I pity the fool.

Squid   You know it.

Leon   Appreciate you coming by.

Squid   Course I come, yer my boy, my blood.

Leon   I know, but cheers.

Squid   Good.

Leon   Look, I'll be done here in a bit. Fancy a night out?

Squid   Doing what?

Leon   Watch a game of footie? See a film?

Squid   Yeah. Leon?

Leon   Let's go see *The Untouchables*. It's at the Odeon.

Squid   Leon, I can't.

Leon   But you like Sean Connery. I hear it's blinding.

Squid   I'm busy.

Leon *sniffs him.*

Squid   Hey!

Leon   That ain't Brut I'm smelling. Old Spice? She must be a right sort if you're getting out the Old Spice.

Squid   You have no idea.

Leon   Yer gonna wind up with big A, the way you carry on.

Squid   I look like Rock Hudson to you?

Leon   So, where is she?

Squid   I have her panting in a bar, cross the road, wid a glass of Babycham. Today of all days I lose my wallet, can you believe?

Leon   No, actually.

Squid   No?

Leon   You blew it on horses, just tell me the truth for once.

Squid   What, you think I would make up a story like that? Come out wid me, come meet her if you think I'm lying, come. Why the hell else would I be here . . . ? I didn't mean that, yeah, yeah?

Leon   Yes, you dd.

Squid   What, so you can read minds now as well as fight? I said I didn't. What, you think I should feel bad?

Leon   I'm not thinking anything.

Squid   Ca I ask you?

Leon   I don't believe this.

Squid   Yer a big man now. You have the whole river to yourself and all I ask for is a lickle summin, not much, but enough to wet my beak. Bwoi, don't look pon me like you want fight me, yeah? You're not in the ring now, Mr High and Mighty . . .

Leon *throws some cash onto the floor.*

Squid   Oh, I see, is that yer game? Want see yer papa on his hands and knees?

Leon   Just go.

Squid   Is who you chat to so? Don't walk away from me, you think you bad, you think you know? I've been here longer than you, child, I know, I know! You know what? Tek yer money. Go shove it up yer white arse!

Leon   Yeah, Dad, good one.

Squid   You know how many people want see Troy bust yer arse tomorrow?

Leon   Let me guess, black people?

Squid   You and yer blasted *shuffle*.

Leon   Well, fuck 'em and fuck you. It's like you always say, Dad, black people, nothing like crabs in a pot. If they can't see what I'm doing for them –

Squid   What the hell do you think you are doing for them?

Leon   Giving them a world champion.

Squid   Yeah, Troy Augustus.

Leon   And I bet you placed money on him.

Squid   Actually, it wass you I betted on. For once. But this is the one time I hope I am wrong. Ca I hope he beats yer living rass. Knock all this *white man* shit out of you.

Leon   This coming from a ponce who spends half his time flying in and out of white minge.

Squid   You can't win.

Leon   I'll take him out in under five, watch me.

Squid   You don't understand, you can't win, neither of you. Why you think all them white people are gonna be there watching you tomorrow night? Ca they love you?

Leon   They do.

Squid   Yer fart. Ca they love nuttin better than see two black men beat up on each other. They too afraid to do it

themselves, so they get you to do it. Love you? Deh the
same people who wanted Tommy to kill you that time. He
was their *white hope*, yer jackarse.

Leon   Bored now.

Squid   Listen, yeah, once you done playing the fool for
them, once they done wid you, you'll realise same as me
this is deh country. You'll be just another wurtless black man
like me.

Leon *shoves* **Squid**.

Squid (*slightly fearful of what his son could do to him next*)
Alright . . . alright.

He leaves the gym quickly.

The ring.

Troy *and* **Leon** *step into the ring and face other.*

Voice of Referee   Right, you know the rules, watch the low
blows, no sucker punches, if there is a knock-down, no
messing about, go straight to your corner and don't come
out till called for. Are we clear? Right, touch gloves, let's go.

Leon *and* **Troy** *retreat to their corners. The bell rings. They fight.*

At first, **Troy** *seems just happy moving around slow, as* **Leon**
dances around him. The crowd are cheering. **Leon** *clips* **Troy**.
Then again, and again, and again.

Charlie   Don't get too close.

Troy *appears not to be trying. He leads* **Leon** *in, then suddenly
lands a punch. He lands another before* **Leon** *realises he was hit
the first time.* **Leon** *is hurt, he stumbles. Crowd are in a frenzy.*

Bell rings.

Second round.

Leon *now seems to be taunting* **Troy**. *Baiting him to catch up with
him as he shuffles around the ring.* **Troy** *loses it. He goes for* **Leon**

who punches back, delivering a sweet right cross. **Troy** *stumbles, he hits the ropes.*

Leon   Thank you and goodnight!

Bell rings.

Leon *and* **Troy** *are in their respective corners.*

Charlie   More like that, keep smoking him out, use your head.

Leon *is hearing but not listening. He cannot keep his eyes off* **Troy***, who is staring back at him, hard.*

Bell rings.

It is the third round. They circle each other again. Without warning, **Troy** *lands five jabs in quick succession.* **Leon** *tries hard to stay on his feet but he is dazed by the quickness of* **Troy***'s delivery. Crowd gasp when* **Leon** *falls to the floor.*

Charlie   Leon! Come on, boy, get up.

Leon *uses what little strength he has left to lift himself up.*

Leon   Is that all you've got, Troy?

Troy *lands a strong left hook, followed by a right one.*

Leon   That all you got?

Troy *lands a few more hooks.*

Leon   What you call that?

Bell rings.

Leon *is breathing heavily.*

Charlie   You can't take another round like that.

Leon   I can beat him.

Charlie   He's killing you.

Leon   I can beat him!

Charlie   Are you sure? Leon, look at me.

Bell rings.

Troy *lands another blow.* **Leon** *is taking hit after hit.*

Leon   Again . . .

Charlie   Leon, your guard.

Leon   Again!

Troy *growls in frustration. None of his blows are knocking out* **Leon**.

Leon *finally throws a punch but it does not land. It misses* **Troy**'s *face by miles.* **Troy** *lands more and more jabs on him.*

Leon   Again. Again. Hit me!

Charlie *can barely look any more. He throws in the towel.*

Bell rings.

Leon   No, no, it was a mistake, he didn't mean it. Charlie, tell him it was as mistake. Pick up the fucking towel, man, tell them it was a mistake! Troy? Come on, Troy, 'e ain't done. Come on, whatever any of you got, I can take it. I can take more, where you going? Troy? Come on. Let's finish this shit right now.

Troy *leaves the ring.*

Leon   Don't you walk away from me, Troy. Don't you walk away. (*Eyes* **Charlie**.) You had to do it. I had him. Where I wanted. Had to do it, Chas, you had to give up. Want people to laugh, call you a joke. Well, not me. Not me. Ain't no loser like you, Charlie, you hearing me, you bloody hearing me? I can take it. You're too much of a pussy to take anything. I can take anything, everything he had, I took. So bring his arse back here. I'm in my prime, I'm ripe! There is nothing I can't take from you, or anyone, nothing. I won, everyone can see it. Bring him back here if you don't believe, bring them all. Everything he had, I can take, take it all, I beat his arse, I can't lose, I won't lose, I just can't. I can't, I can't, I won't be like you!

Charlie *leaves the ring*.

Leon   Yeah, run away again, Chas, go on! Run as fast! (*Calls*.) I won't be like you! I can take more. I can take more. I can take more.

Leon *paces around the ring. He exhausts himself. He holds his head in his hands as he drops to his knees in the middle of the ring*.

Leon *is back in the gym. Still on his knees. Bailiff's men are coming in and out. Taking away the equipment.* **Troy** *enters*.

Troy   Loser cleans the bogs.

Leon   What? What did you say?

Troy   I said, loser cleans the bogs. Winner mops the floor.

Leon   You remember?

Troy   Yeah, I remember. Toilets still bad here?

Leon   Like you wouldn't believe.

Bailiff's men come in, removing the equipment.

Troy   They still missing the bowl?

Leon   Even when they have a crap.

Troy (*disgusted*)   Oh man!

Leon   You know it.

Troy   I don't want to hear that.

Leon   That's white boys for you.

Troy/Leon   Nasty.

Troy   So, what's happening?

Leon   The gym's closed, Troy. Charlie's had it. He only went and put every penny we had in the stock market.

Troy   Shit, that's gotta hurt. But you're still here?

Leon What else am I gonna do?

Troy Good. Cos there is a toilet bowl in there with your name on it. Come on, Leon, admit it to yourself, I whupped yer ass.

Leon Is that why you came here?

Troy Tell me.

Leon What did you expect me to do, Troy?

Troy Just tell me.

Leon Back then, years ago, what did you expect me to do?

Troy What are you talking –

Leon Stop lying to me. Just stop it. What did you want me to do?

Troy (*snaps*) You ran! Like the *white boy* you are, you ran.

Leon What was I supposed to do?

Troy Throw a brick? Fight them off?

Leon There was loads of them.

Troy Stand there and piss your pants for all I care, but don't leave me!

Leon I was scared.

Troy I was scared without you.

Leon You've lost your accent, Troy.

Troy (*puts on London accent*) *Yeah, you know what I mean?*

He does his take of the Leon Shuffle.

Troy What you think?

Leon Not bad.

Troy Faster than you?

Leon Almost as fast.

Troy   Oh yes?

The boys jump like they are on springs. They begin playfully sparring around the gym. They are clearly enjoying each other's company.

Leon   Come on, brown sugar, scared I'll catch yer?

Troy   You couldn't catch a cold, you Black Mariah.

They laugh. This banter reminds them both of happier times.

Ray *enters.*

Ray   Troy? What do you think you're doing?

Troy   It's alright, man.

Ray   No, it's not alright. What the hell?

Troy   We're just fooling, be cool.

Ray   Fuck cool.

Troy   Yo, Ray, come on.

Ray   Those hands of yours are insured for a hundred grand, each.

Troy   Hold up.

Ray   You don't even have gloves on, what the fuck?

Troy   Like I'm trying to explain to you, if you let me, it's not for real.

Ray   Get outta there. Get yer ass over here now! Nigga, you deaf?

Troy *does as he is told and steps out of the ring.*

Ray   What the fuck is wrong with you?

Troy   I'm sorry.

Ray   Sorry is for losers. Don't ever do that shit again. Cab's waiting. Come on. Let's go, babe! We got a plane.

Troy   Hold up.

Ray   For what?

Troy   Have a heart, Ray?

Ray   A heart? For who? Oh Jeez. (*To* **Leon**.) Take yer ass-whupping like a man, fool! You're British, should be used to that.

Troy   Ray, you're not helping.

Ray   Let's go, babe. World-title fight is ours for the taking now! You know how much money we are talking here?

Troy   Ray?

Ray   Time for fresh meat, and his name is Rollins. And we want him sweating like a pig who knows he's dinner. Move on, boy. Get yer punk ass in the car.

Troy   You know, you don't talk to me that way.

Ray   I will talk anyway I goddam please! *You* don't talk to me this way, *you* don't talk anyway, until *I* say the hell say so.

Troy   I don't belong to you.

Ray   You want to walk?

Troy   Don't push me.

Ray   I found you. I made you. Now I am cold as a motherfucker and I am as hungry as a bear, and the sooner I get out of this miserable country, the better it is for my health. Don't you ever, in yer *life*, give me shit about you want to walk. I own your ticket in case you forget. You and I are in bed, so you speak when I tell you. You fight who I tell you. You are mine. Now for the last goddam time, get in the fucking car, bitch. Right now, let's go.

Troy   One minute.

Ray   You got five seconds, starting now. Time for fresh meat.

He leaves.

(*Off.*) Troy?

Leon   Do as the Yank man says, is it, Troy?

Troy   I'm sorry, Leon.

Troy *leaves.*

Leon *spars by himself.*

Charlie *staggers out of his office, nursing a hangover.* **Leon** *sees him.*

Charlie   Why are you still here? Eh? I thought you couldn't stand the sight of me any more.

Leon   Correct.

Charlie   Come on, get out, it's time to go. I said get out. Leon? The bailiffs are outside, they want the keys.

Leon   So, give it to them . . .

Charlie   Well, if you wouldn't mind?

Leon (*sneers*)   Piss-artist.

Charlie   Oi! You know you can't stay here.

Leon   Watch me.

Charlie   I'm not in the mood for this. Leon, I mean it.

Leon   I'm not going.

Charlie   Get the fuck out.

Leon   No.

Charlie   You can't stay here.

Leon   Where am I supposed to go, Chas, tell me?

Charlie   That's not my problem any more.

Leon   Where do I go, what do I do?

Charlie   I need to leave.

Leon   Bloody go then.

Charlie   Before this place kills me altogether. Don't you understand that?

Leon   Just leave me here.

Charlie *watches as* **Leon** *resumes sparring by himself.*

Charlie   I can't do that. Leon? Will you please let me leave? It's over, boy! It's all over. We lost. Are you receiving? Do you think I want this to happen? This was my gym, this was my home.

Leon (*mimics*)   Good old Maggie.

Charlie   Don't you make fun of me. Now come out of there. Look, don't make me call the police on yer, cos I bloody will this time, boy.

Leon   Is that all I am, Chas? Your *boy*?

Charlie   Well, what else? You tell me.

Leon   Nothing.

Charlie   Nothing?

Leon   Don't you get it?

Charlie   What are you talking about? You'll be alright, you're young. Another gym, new trainer, you'll be fighting again in no time. No scrap heap for you.

Leon   Chas, I am done with it.

Charlie   Don't say that.

Leon   I am.

Charlie   That's silly talk.

Leon *extends his hands.*

Charlie   No. No, Leon, you can't.

Leon   Please, Chas.

Charlie   You're a fighter!

He accepts the inevitable. He helps **Leon** *takes of his gloves and the hand wrap.*

Charlie   So, what do you think you are going to do now?

Leon   I dunno.

Charlie   You scared?

Leon   Yeah, I am.

Charlie   You should be. I'll be outside

He jumps out of the ring and leaves. Before leaving, he places the gloves on the side of the ring. One last attempt to change **Leon***'s mind.*

Charlie   You'll be back.

He leaves the gym. **Leon** *goes to his locker and puts on a pair of jogging pants and a new shirt. He grabs his bag, walks past the ring and picks up the gloves* **Charlie** *left. He throws them straight into the bin.* **Leon** *then walks slowly out of the gym for the very last time, turning off the lights as he goes.*

Blackout.

Methuen Drama Student Editions

Jean Anouilh *Antigone* • John Arden *Serjeant Musgrave's Dance*
Alan Ayckbourn *Confusions* • Aphra Behn *The Rover* • Edward Bond
Lear • *Saved* • Bertolt Brecht *The Caucasian Chalk Circle* • *Fear and
Misery in the Third Reich* • *The Good Person of Szechwan* • *Life of Galileo* •
Mother Courage and her Children • *The Resistible Rise of Arturo Ui* • *The
Threepenny Opera* • Anton Chekhov *The Cherry Orchard* • *The Seagull* •
Three Sisters • *Uncle Vanya* • Caryl Churchill *Serious Money* • *Top Girls*
• Shelagh Delaney *A Taste of Honey* • Euripides *Elektra* • *Medea* •
Dario Fo *Accidental Death of an Anarchist* • Michael Frayn *Copenhagen*
• John Galsworthy *Strife* • Nikolai Gogol *The Government Inspector* •
Robert Holman *Across Oka* • Henrik Ibsen *A Doll's House* • *Ghosts* •
Hedda Gabler • Charlotte Keatley *My Mother Said I Never Should* •
Bernard Kops *Dreams of Anne Frank* • Federico García Lorca *Blood
Wedding* • *Doña Rosita the Spinster* (bilingual edition) • *The House of
Bernarda Alba* • (bilingual edition) • *Yerma* (bilingual edition) • David
Mamet *Glengarry Glen Ross* • *Oleanna* • Patrick Marber *Closer* • John
Marston *Malcontent* • Martin McDonagh *The Lieutenant of Inishmore* •
Joe Orton *Loot* • Luigi Pirandello *Six Characters in Search of an Author*
• Mark Ravenhill *Shopping and F***ing* • Willy Russell *Blood Brothers*
• *Educating Rita* • Sophocles *Antigone* • *Oedipus the King* • Wole
Soyinka *Death and the King's Horseman* • Shelagh Stephenson *The
Memory of Water* • August Strindberg *Miss Julie* • J. M. Synge *The
Playboy of the Western World* • Theatre Workshop *Oh What a Lovely
War* Timberlake Wertenbaker *Our Country's Good* • Arnold Wesker
The Merchant • Oscar Wilde *The Importance of Being Earnest* •
Tennessee Williams *A Streetcar Named Desire* • *The Glass Menagerie*

Methuen Drama Modern Plays

include work by

Edward Albee
Jean Anouilh
John Arden
Margaretta D'Arcy
Peter Barnes
Sebastian Barry
Brendan Behan
Dermot Bolger
Edward Bond
Bertolt Brecht
Howard Brenton
Anthony Burgess
Simon Burke
Jim Cartwright
Caryl Churchill
Complicite
Noël Coward
Lucinda Coxon
Sarah Daniels
Nick Darke
Nick Dear
Shelagh Delaney
David Edgar
David Eldridge
Dario Fo
Michael Frayn
John Godber
Paul Godfrey
David Greig
John Guare
Peter Handke
David Harrower
Jonathan Harvey
Iain Heggie
Declan Hughes
Terry Johnson
Sarah Kane
Charlotte Keatley
Barrie Keeffe

Howard Korder
Robert Lepage
Doug Lucie
Martin McDonagh
John McGrath
Terrence McNally
David Mamet
Patrick Marber
Arthur Miller
Mtwa, Ngema & Simon
Tom Murphy
Phyllis Nagy
Peter Nichols
Sean O'Brien
Joseph O'Connor
Joe Orton
Louise Page
Joe Penhall
Luigi Pirandello
Stephen Poliakoff
Franca Rame
Mark Ravenhill
Philip Ridley
Reginald Rose
Willy Russell
Jean-Paul Sartre
Sam Shepard
Wole Soyinka
Simon Stephens
Shelagh Stephenson
Peter Straughan
C. P. Taylor
Theatre Workshop
Sue Townsend
Judy Upton
Timberlake Wertenbaker
Roy Williams
Snoo Wilson
Victoria Wood

Methuen Drama Modern Classics

Methuen Drama Contemporary Dramatists
include

John Arden (two volumes)
Arden & D'Arcy
Peter Barnes (three volumes)
Sebastian Barry
Dermot Bolger
Edward Bond (eight volumes)
Howard Brenton
  (two volumes)
Richard Cameron
Jim Cartwright
Caryl Churchill (two volumes)
Sarah Daniels (two volumes)
Nick Darke
David Edgar (three volumes)
David Eldridge
Ben Elton
Dario Fo (two volumes)
Michael Frayn (three volumes)
David Greig
John Godber (four volumes)
Paul Godfrey
John Guare
Lee Hall (two volumes)
Peter Handke
Jonathan Harvey
  (two volumes)
Declan Hughes
Terry Johnson (three volumes)
Sarah Kane
Barrie Keeffe
Bernard-Marie Koltès
  (two volumes)
Franz Xaver Kroetz
David Lan
Bryony Lavery
Deborah Levy
Doug Lucie

David Mamet (four volumes)
Martin McDonagh
Duncan McLean
Anthony Minghella
  (two volumes)
Tom Murphy (six volumes)
Phyllis Nagy
Anthony Neilsen (two volumes)
Philip Osment
Gary Owen
Louise Page
Stewart Parker (two volumes)
Joe Penhall (two volumes)
Stephen Poliakoff
  (three volumes)
David Rabe (two volumes)
Mark Ravenhill (two volumes)
Christina Reid
Philip Ridley
Willy Russell
Eric-Emmanuel Schmitt
Ntozake Shange
Sam Shepard (two volumes)
Wole Soyinka (two volumes)
Simon Stephens (two volumes)
Shelagh Stephenson
David Storey (three volumes)
Sue Townsend
Judy Upton
Michel Vinaver
  (two volumes)
Arnold Wesker (two volumes)
Michael Wilcox
Roy Williams (three volumes)
Snoo Wilson (two volumes)
David Wood (two volumes)
Victoria Wood

Methuen Drama Classical Greek Dramatists

Aeschylus Plays: One
(Persians, Seven Against Thebes, Suppliants,
Prometheus Bound)

Aeschylus Plays: Two
(Oresteia: Agamemnon, Libation-Bearers, Eumenides)

Aristophanes Plays: One
(Acharnians, Knights, Peace, Lysistrata)

Aristophanes Plays: Two
(Wasps, Clouds, Birds, Festival Time, Frogs)

Aristophanes & Menander: New Comedy
(Women in Power, Wealth, The Malcontent,
The Woman from Samos)

Euripides Plays: One
(Medea, The Phoenician Women, Bacchae)

Euripides Plays: Two
(Hecuba, The Women of Troy, Iphigeneia at Aulis,
Cyclops)

Euripides Plays: Three
(Alkestis, Helen, Ion)

Euripides Plays: Four
(Elektra, Orestes, Iphigeneia in Tauris)

Euripides Plays: Five
(Andromache, Herakles' Children, Herakles)

Euripides Plays: Six
(Hippolytos, Suppliants, Rhesos)

Sophocles Plays: One
(Oedipus the King, Oedipus at Colonus, Antigone)

Sophocles Plays: Two
(Ajax, Women of Trachis, Electra, Philoctetes)